Case Closed:

Ian Bailey and the Murder of Sophie Toscan du Plantier

Case Closed:

Ian Bailey and the Murder of Sophie Toscan du Plantier

PAUL MORGAN

*Case Closed: Ian Bailey and the
Murder of Sophie Toscan du Plantier*
Copyright © Paul Morgan 2024

Published in the United Kingdom 2024

All rights reserved
This book is sold subject to the condition that it shall not, by way of trade or otherwise, be hired out, lent or resold, or otherwise circulated without the author's/publisher's prior consent in any form of binding or cover other than that in which it is published and without a similar condition including this condition being imposed on the subsequent publisher.

The moral rights of the author have been asserted.

Contents

Part one - Becoming the prime suspect 1

Introduction: Three women, three statements, and Bailey's guilt 3

Chapter 1   He did it 11

Chapter 2   How Bailey made himself the prime suspect from the beginning 15

Chapter 3   Two contradictory narratives: Both cannot be true 45

Chapter 4   80 minutes - Caught in a trap of his own making 59

Chapter 5   Aftermath – Post 2001 The ever-developing case against Ian Bailey 75

Chapter 6   December 21st to 23rd 1996 - reasonable inferences 85

Part two - The growing evidence against Ian Bailey 99

Chapter 7   The case of the disappearing and reappearing scratches 101

Chapter 8   The case of the invisible confessions 121

Chapter 9   Bailey knew Sophie 137

Part three - A Betrayal of Justice? 151
Introduction - The analysis of the DPP Report **2001** 153
Chapter 10 The 'prosecution' of AGS 159
Chapter 11 Aftermath 2 Post-2001 187
Chapter 12 Inconsistencies in relation to Bailey's
                response to Garda questioning
                (Report section 6) 199
Chapter 13 Scratches, Confessions,
                and Did Bailey Know Sophie 223
Chapter 14 Bailey's alleged incriminating knowledge
                of the murder (Report section 11) 247
Chapter 15 Alleged similar fact evidence and
                sexual motive (Report section 15) 257
Case Closed **267**
Appendices
1. The chronology of Ian Bailey's involvement
   in the Sophie Toscan du Plantier case 271
2. Statements indicating Bailey's guilt,
   including over 60 excluded or severely
   minimised regarding the 2001 DPP report 275
3. A sample of assumptions and assertions
   in the DPP 2001 report..285
4. The remaining DPP sections 297
5. Some questions for Jules Thomas..............................309

Thank you, Michelle Cawley, for outstanding research on the statements and documents. On many occasions, you uncovered evidence that demonstrated Ian Bailey's guilt. The book is far better because of your contributions.

Book cover 'My mother's blood has entered (Irish) soil' photograph by Tina Conroy

"My Mother's Blood Has Entered (Irish) Soil"

Sophie Toscan du Plantier was murdered on December 23rd, 1996. She died close to her remote Irish holiday cottage. It was a place where she had been happy and contented. At times with family, friends and sometimes alone. In the early hours of the morning, Sophie suffered a frenzied, brutal, and sustained attack.

The Office of the Director of Public Prosecutions' decision in 2001 and thereafter was that there was insufficient evidence to bring criminal charges against Ian Bailey. This intensified and prolonged the suffering of the people who loved Sophie. Many people in Ireland believed that the failure to charge Bailey was a gross injustice.

The woman-hating paedophile drank and drugged himself into an early grave. He died penniless, after several heart attacks, lying in a gutter outside his temporary accommodation. No one wept for him or attended his pauper's cremation. He spent much of his last few years wandering the streets of Bantry tramp-like, pushing an old empty supermarket trolley, trying to scrounge free drinks from tourists or hidden away in his room, making lists of people he hated and writing curses about them. His books of poetry were so atrocious they made illiteracy a blessing. It was a life marked by abject failure.

An enduring feature of those who supported the murderer was that they had not seen most of the evidence gathered on Ian Bailey. Their defence amounted to regurgitating gossip and peddling lies. The pro-pervert and AGS-hating conspiracy theorists had been firing blanks for decades. No amount of their 'shouting,' threats, or endless repetition of lies could show Bailey to be innocent.

Far more concerning than the ignorance of Bailey's useful idiots was the decision reached by the Office of the Director of Public Prosecutions. They had all the information and concluded that Bailey had no case to answer. The report that prevented Bailey from going on trial excluded dozens of important statements while including many evidence-free assumptions made in favour of Bailey. When the full facts are included and groundless assumptions are ignored, the case against Ian Bailey is compelling.

When Sophie's son said, "My mother's blood has entered (Irish) soil," it was true, both literally and figuratively. Many people in Ireland who never met Sophie care about her and her family and want justice for them.

I hope this book will, in some small way, bring justice a little closer.

Paul Morgan

PART ONE
Becoming the prime suspect

Introduction: Three Women, Three Statements, And Bailey's Guilt

Ian Bailey murdered Sophie Toscan du Plantier. An objective and reasoned evaluation of the evidence can lead only to that conclusion. In this book, you will learn about dozens of police statements concerning the murder of Sophie Toscan du Plantier that have been unknown to most people for over 25 years. They will reveal why An Garda Síochána knew they had a very strong case against Ian Bailey. The statements will help people to understand why Ian Bailey was found guilty of murder by a French court in 2019.

Part one will present a detailed analysis of the evidence showing how Ian Bailey repeatedly lied to investigators and, in doing so, became the prime suspect. It will also show how the statements of dozens of other people can be pieced together to expose Bailey's culpability for the murder. The second part of the book will explore three important topics in the murder case: scratches, confessions, and whether Bailey knew Sophie. For each topic, the evidence points towards Bailey's guilt.

In the final part of the book, Betrayal of Justice?, the Office of the Director of Public Prosecutions (DPP) decision will be scrutinized. In a 2001 report, the DPP concluded,

'A prosecution against Bailey is not warranted by the evidence.' This decision meant Bailey never stood trial in Ireland. You will see that dozens of important statements were excluded from the DPP Report, while many unjustifiable assumptions and inferences were given prominence. This resulted in Bailey avoiding a trial in which he would most likely have been convicted. The decision reached by the report author, Robert Sheehan, and the DPP has caused decades of terrible suffering for the son, parents, extended family, and friends of Sophie Toscan du Plantier. For many people, it has also been a blight on the Irish legal system.

In this brief introduction, the evidence of three women will highlight why Bailey was culpable. It will not present the full statements made by these women. Instead, in each case, it will be a key revelation that is found in their evidence to investigators. All the women were well known to Bailey. There are important similarities in all these statements. The witnesses have never varied their statements. The only person contradicting these women was Ian Bailey. Their statements have been corroborated by independent parties. Ian Bailey has no such corroboration, it is just his word and nothing else.

The first woman is Shirley Foster. She discovered Sophie's body on the morning of December 23rd, 1996. She lived in a detached cottage adjacent to the one owned by her French neighbour. Foster and her partner, Alfie Lyons, knew Sophie, and they were also friends of Ian Bailey and Jules Thomas. The second woman is Jules Thomas, Bailey's long-term partner for over twenty-five years. The third is Saffron Thomas the eldest daughter of Jules Thomas.

Introduction: Three Women, Three Statements, And Bailey's Guilt

The statements

When the women were interviewed by French investigators in 2011, they had the right to have legal counsel present. The interviews were recorded and signed off by the interviewee in each case.

1. He knew about the death before anyone else. Saffron Thomas to the French investigators in 2011

Saffron Thomas confirmed that she spoke to her mother, Jules Thomas, between 11 am and 12 pm on December 23rd, 1996. This was over 100 minutes earlier than the time Jules Thomas claimed she was told about the death by Bailey, following his conversation with Eddie Cassidy. It is close to the time Jules Thomas told James Camier about the death in Dreenane.

> "Called JT on the 23rd wanting a lift, "probably about 11 or 12". "She (JT) said on the phone there had been a murder and she had either "been there or was going there"
>
> Saffron Thomas 2011

This meant Jules Thomas knew about the murder on the morning of the 23rd. She would have known it when she left her home at or before 10 am. So, she and Bailey knew about the death before the body was discovered, approximately 40 minutes before the Garda arrived at the scene of the crime, and hours before a doctor confirmed the woman was deceased. Saffron Thomas made her original statement on this issue in 2002. It came after the original DPP report but would have been presented to the office. The DPP decided it was not significant.

2. He knew where the murder took place. Shirley Foster to the French investigators in 2011

Foster has always insisted that she met Bailey and Thomas on Dreenane Lane on December 23rd, 1996. Something that Jules Thomas has always corroborated. This confirms that Ian Bailey knew where to find the deceased woman. He said he knew exactly where to go in his 31.12.1996 statement. He had no legitimate way of knowing where to find the deceased. In an article written for the Irish Times by Dick Hogan in January 1997, it stated that the gardai found that 410 non-nationals were living in the area. Despite this, Bailey drives straight to an obscure holiday home. Moreover, he went there without checking with his friends, Sophie's nearest neighbours, that a crime had been committed in that place.

> "Subsequently, he lied about it. Later, he said that he had met me at the intersection when in reality, we crossed each other halfway between the intersection and the house, at the bend."
>
> Shirley Foster 2011

Bailey and Thomas met Foster partway down Dreenane Lane. He had driven down the lane many times. He knew it led to the cottages and no further. If he was on the lane he was going to the cottages. When he said he knew exactly where to go, he did. Bailey gives the same account as Foster and Thomas in his early statements. Later, he tried several times to claim that he had not driven directly to the scene of the crime. He was lying in an attempt to hide the incriminating truth.

3. He knew the identity of the victim.
Jules Thomas to the French investigators in 2011

In her 2011 statement, Thomas re-affirms information she had provided fifteen years earlier. All of it is damning for Ian Bailey. This included her statements on what she and Bailey did after a brief visit to the scene of the crime. They left and drove to the post office in Toormore. In the original statements, there was full agreement between Bailey, Thomas, and the two post office workers, Ann Dukelow and Nan Jermyn. Bailey went there to get the name of the dead French woman who owned a holiday home in Dreenane. Soon, Bailey would claim he went to the post office without a specific objective, and only on arriving there did someone else volunteer the name of the victim.

Dukelow, and Jermyn stood by their original story, and Thomas confirmed it in 2011

> "We weren't sure of her name. We then went to the post office in Toormore and asked the postwoman if she knew the name of the person who lived next door to Alfie Lyons. She said she thought it was BOUNIOL. It must have been around 2.30-3.00 p.m."
>
> Jules Thomas 2011

There was nothing to suggest to Bailey that the dead woman in Dreenane must be Sophie. He never explained why he knew she owned the cottage in 1996, did not explain why he knew she was there just before Christmas, nor how he knew the body was that of Sophie. It was possible that Sophie was there with other women or that she had let friends, including other women, use the cottage. With other women at the cottage, it was impossible to be certain who was dead. Despite all these potential unknowns, he did not make any attempt to find out who it may be. He went to the post office and requested the name of the cottage owner.

There is no reason to disbelieve these three pieces of evidence and the corroboration from over a dozen witnesses. This means Bailey knew about the murder many hours before he says he was told. He therefore lied about when he claimed he learned of the death. He knew the exact location of the crime scene and drove straight there. Finally, he knew who the victim was, as he drove to the Post Office. Not only did he have all this guilty knowledge, he sought to cover it up by lying.

He knew about the murder before everyone else; he knew where the murder had taken place, and he knew who the victim was.

Three women, three statements, and Bailey's guilt.

Appendix 1 The chronology of events

CHAPTER **1**

He did it

In the early hours of 23rd December 1996, Sophie Toscan du Plantier was brutally and savagely murdered close to her holiday home. Her cottage was one of 3 hidden away in an obscure area called Dreenane, West Cork. She was murdered by an Englishman who lived in the area, a man named Ian Kenneth Bailey. The naming of Bailey is not idle speculation. The evidence against him is overwhelming; he has been convicted of the murder, and this book will explain why that was the correct decision.

The overwhelming majority of authors and serious journalists writing about the case have concluded Bailey did it. The Irish Police force reached the same conclusion. Most significantly, a French trial in 2019 found him guilty of the murder.

The evidence

Evidence means anything that can be admitted to prove or disprove alleged matters of facts in a trial. The evidence may be presented verbally or in documents (written). This evidence can be divided into two subcategories: direct evidence and circumstantial evidence. Whatever the forms of evidence presented, the ultimate question for a jury is the same: Has the prosecution provided enough evidence so that the jury or Judges are sure that the defendant is guilty?

Direct and Circumstantial Evidence

Direct evidence is facts that directly support the truth of an assertion without intervening inference. Eyewitness testimony is direct evidence. It consists of a witness's description of their reputed direct sensory experience of events with no presentation of additional facts. Direct evidence links a person and a crime and demonstrates the ultimate fact to be proved.

Circumstantial evidence necessitates some reasoning or inference to prove a fact. This type of evidence is sometimes called "indirect evidence." In many situations, more than one piece of circumstantial evidence will be used to draw the judge or jury to a specific conclusion that stands alone. It is possible that a single piece of circumstantial evidence can strongly suggest something. A person may draw inferences about either a fact or an event that took place.

Circumstantial evidence is real evidence. It relies on a person making an inference to connect it to a conclusion of fact. We use inference many times a day. We would be stuck without it. A fingerprint at the scene of the crime does not prove a person committed that crime. However, it enables people to infer that a particular person was at a certain location at some time. When combined with other circumstantial evidence, it can make a compelling case.

One of the most ill-informed reasons Bailey's supporters use to condemn the French Court's decision is the 'lack of hard evidence.' The people saying this rarely have a definition of the various types of evidence. Often, they apply a random 'CSI television programme's point of view.' The same people fail to understand that DNA and fingerprint evidence are circumstantial. It is scientific evidence presented by an expert that enables jurors to draw conclusions.

A single piece of circumstantial evidence may allow for more than one explanation. A circumstantial case is built through the accumulation of evidence. The many pieces of evidence and consistent inferences can make a case stronger and compelling. Alternative explanations may be investigated and disproven.

In a circumstantial case, jury members or Judges may reasonably conclude that people are lying. Further conclusions will be drawn about those who lie repeatedly or who change their stories in the face of new evidence. Likewise, people presenting false alibis that are subsequently disproven enable observers to make inferences about the deception.

Different pieces of circumstantial evidence may be required, each corroborating the conclusions drawn from the others. When combined, they may more strongly support one particular inference over another. The prosecution seeks to combine separate events and circumstances that can be explained rationally only by the defendant's guilt.

In law, in a circumstantial case, there is an understanding that in most cases, there is an unlikelihood of chance or coincidence. Combining different parts of the evidence may eventually eliminate all other possible outcomes.

In the case of the murder of Sophie Toscan du Plantier, the weight of the evidence is compelling. Ian Bailey was the murderer.

CHAPTER **2**

How Bailey made himself the prime suspect from the beginning

Bailey's initial 1996 version of what happened the night Sophie Toscan du Plantier was murdered

The heading refers to the initial Bailey version because it was the first of many versions he offered following the murder. All of them were full of deception and lies. This industrial-scale dishonesty was driven by two factors; the first came when Bailey was caught telling lies. He would respond with new lies and false narratives. The second factor came when Bailey told truths that directly implicated him regarding the murder. He would then concoct new lies in an attempt to put distance between himself and the truth. In part one, the dozens of lies will be pointed out. It is a sorry affair.

On the evening of December 21ˢᵗ and the morning of the 22ⁿᵈ

Ian Bailey told the AGS investigators that he was at home on the evening and night of Saturday 21ˢᵗ. He said that on the morning of the 22ⁿᵈ, he chopped down the top of a Spruce tree in preparation for the Christmas holiday. Bailey claimed that he was helped by Saffron Thomas. Then, at lunchtime, he said he killed three turkeys. Bailey explained that he used a bow saw to cut down the tree and cut himself in the process.

The evening of the 22ⁿᵈ

Bailey and Thomas said they drove into Schull for an evening of drinking. In their original statements, they both informed the Police that around midnight, they left the Courtyard bar and drove straight home by the usual and shortest route. They went straight from the Courtyard to the Prairie cottage. They did not stop or leave the car. Soon after they arrived home, they both went to bed after 1 a.m. They remained in bed throughout the night.

The morning of the 23ʳᵈ

Bailey explained that on the morning of the 23ʳᵈ, between 8 am and 9 am *1, he made coffee for himself and Jules Thomas. He returned to bed. He and Thomas lay in bed drinking coffee, listening to the radio, and making plans for the afternoon. Bailey said he spent the rest of the morning and early afternoon 'pottering about'. He made no reference to leaving the cottage nor to making or receiving phone calls. His reference to 'pottering about' was all he said to describe his time from being in bed at approximately 10 am through to getting a phone call from the journalist Eddie Cassidy at 1.40 pm

The call and the following eighty minutes

Ian Bailey claimed that Eddie Cassidy told him a French woman had been murdered in Toormore, and he wanted him to investigate. Despite these alleged general points, Bailey was adamant that he knew exactly where to go to find the scene of the crime*2. He made no reference to making or receiving any calls between the call from Cassidy and driving directly to Dreenane, which did turn out to be the place of the death.

While driving to the scene of the crime, Ian Bailey met Shirley Foster on Dreenane Lane. The only place the lane runs to are a few cottages in Dreenane; it goes nowhere else. This proved he did indeed know exactly where to go. He did not ask Foster or the Gards any detailed journalistic questions. It is not that any of them refused to answer questions; he did not ask any. This was strange behaviour coming from an investigative journalist.

Within a matter of minutes, Bailey and Thomas set off for the local Post office. On arriving, he asked the staff for the name of the murdered French woman who owned

> a cottage in Dreenane*3. Soon after, he returned to the Prairie cottage.
>
> This was the version given by Bailey to investigators up to and including his main statement on 31.12.1996.
>
> As you are about to see, it was a tissue of lies, and those lies point directly to Bailey's guilt.
>
> *1 corroborated by Jules Thomas but changed when revealed as a false alibi
>
> *2 corroborated by others but changed by Bailey when the truth of it implicated him
>
> *3 corroborated by others but changed by Bailey when the truth of it implicated him

The timeline

An important part of the investigation of a murder like this one is to establish a timeline. This necessitates interviewing all the people who were in the area of the murder at the time of the crime and the time immediately before and after it. Each person in the vicinity is required to explain what they were doing, where they were doing it, and when they were doing it during the period specified by senior officers. This provides investigators with a detailed picture of people's activities. It can isolate any gaps in a timeline. It can check whether a person's story is corroborated or contradicted by the statements of others. It is an invaluable investigative tool.

If officers detect gaps, they may inquire further. If there are contradictions, they need to be clarified. Ultimately, contradictions can expose mistakes, and more importantly, they may reveal lies. The investigators will focus more closely on people who are caught lying in statements.

After the murder of Sophie, one statement from hundreds taken was given by local inhabitant Ian Bailey. An Englishman who had moved to Ireland in the early 1990s. He was at the time living in the home, the Prairie cottage, of Welsh artist Jules Thomas and her daughters. In the UK he worked as a journalist and was starting to do work as a freelance journalist in West Cork. He had been picking up a lot of work following the murder of Sophie. Bailey was a man who boasted of having an excellent memory and being a fastidious journalist. If anyone could give An Garda Síochána police officers a precise statement, it should be him.

The early lies told by Bailey on Christmas weekend

Ian Bailey relentlessly lied to investigators about the entire weekend before Sophie's murder. This is most notable concerning the evening of the 21st, the morning of the 22nd, and when Bailey and Thomas travel back to the Prairie cottage in the early hours of December 23rd. Many of Bailey's lies were exposed when he changed his own story. When he tells contradictory tales, some or all of what he says must be untrue.

21.12.1996 and the morning of 22.12.1996

In his 31.12.1996 statement, Bailey did not mention being in Schull overnight on the night of the 21st. Instead, he implied he had stayed at the cottage. He told investigators that on the morning of the 22nd, he and Saffron cut down a Christmas tree, and then at lunchtime, he killed three turkeys. However, this was a tissue of lies. He was being dishonest. The true story was that Bailey stayed in Schull on the night of the 21st, drinking excessively. He arranged to sleep at the home of an associate's mother, Mrs Murphy. While at the house he spoke to mutual friends who were staying there and the family of his associate. Close to lunchtime the following day he walked to the newsagents to buy some newspapers. Eventually, he got a lift to the Prairie cottage.

The scale of these falsehoods is significant. This is not the case of Ian Bailey getting the time wrong by an hour or two when giving a statement a year after the event. He gets everything wrong within days of the event. Furthermore, this narrative was not changed because Bailey suddenly realised the truth and immediately told the investigators of his error. He must have realised that everyone was being interviewed, including all the people in the Murphy household, on the night of 21.12.1996. It was only after Bailey checked to see if others there that night had mentioned him in their statements, they had, did he come clean with AGS. Bailey was 'forced' to come clean and give a more truthful account.

It defies credulity that Bailey had forgotten what he had done for a full 15-18 hours. How could anyone believe that being out in bars, socialising with many people, sleeping on someone's sofa, going for a newspaper, having brews, and getting a lift home had slipped the memory of this experienced journalist?

This will be the first of many times when Bailey gives a statement and then completely changes his story after being exposed. It will become apparent that Bailey lies frequently and effortlessly. The pattern of behaviour is to lie and, when found out, produce some new lies. The unanswered question is: why did Bailey choose to lie to AGS so comprehensively about his activities? He was seeking to hide something, but it is unlikely that we will ever know his intention. What is known is that he lied about his activities that night and the following morning.

The journey home in the early hours of 23.12.1996

There were also false statements about the journey home from Schull between 00.00 and 00.30 a.m. on December 23rd. He initially said that he and Thomas left the Courtyard bar and took the most direct route home. Bailey said he was driving, and they went directly home without stopping. Jules Thomas confirmed this timeline of events.

However, Bailey and Thomas soon changed every item of that narrative. It transpired that they actually left the Galley bar. They did not take the most direct route home. Instead, they opted for a more scenic journey home. Furthermore, in truth, they did not drive straight home without stopping. They stopped at Hunt's Hill. Not only did Bailey pull up there he also decided to exit the vehicle and look across the valley in the direction of the cottages in Dreenane. One of the cottages was Sophie's. It was likely that he took that route home so that he could stop and look across the valley. At trial, he would be asked to explain why.

The couple gave the same inaccurate story in their first version of events. Soon afterward, they told a completely different version. Once again, the couple corroborated each other. It seemed that each of them could not keep their simple story straight. On both occasions, they were in sync. They agreed on inaccurate statements. This type of odd behaviour is a 'red flag' to investigators. If the first version of events was inaccurate, one must ask why that was so. Are the lies told to cover up something? In a trial, Bailey would need to explain why he drove to a spot that overlooked Dreenane, got out of the car, and looked toward the cottages. Those cottages would be the scene of a horrific murder only a few hours later. He would have been expected to explain why he covered up all these activities.

These falsehoods and contradictions were clear-cut examples of deceptive behaviour. Bailey's substantial statement on December 31st revealed more lies and dishonesty. Part three of this book will show how the Office of the Director of Public Prosecutions did not think these lies were worth addressing.

The events of 23.12.1996, according to Bailey's 31.12.1996 statement

The 31.12.1996 statement Bailey gave and signed was five pages long. It was taken at the Prairie Cottage, Toormore, Co Cork, by Detective Garda JP Culligan and Detective Garda D Harrington. Much of the statement covered his basic personal details and some previous history. He then moved on to matters relating to the crime in the statement.

He explained how he learned about the death and his actions thereafter. Four key parts of the statement are presented below, not in the order they came in within the statement but in the chronological order of what Bailey said he did during the relevant period. What Bailey signed off on eight days after the murder explains why he so quickly became the prime suspect. (All the quotations from statements are produced as they were documented. Sometimes, there were misspellings, and these were not amended.)

Excerpts from the statement:

1

Regarding December 22nd Bailey and his scratches

"Marks/Scratches.

Climbed up a 20 ft tree to cut the top off for Xmas. Sunday morning 22.12.1996 accompanied by Saffy Thomas (23). Dragged tree up lane and met a fellow Sullivan with horse and cart. (Big round man). Cut with bow saw, cuts healed."

> 2
>
> Regarding December 22nd through to around 1.30am on the 23rd
>
> "Sunday 22.12.1996 about lunch time killed 3 turkeys. At home with Jules until 9p.m. and then went to Courtyard in my Fiesta. Stayed there until 12m.n. Quinlan behind bar, John - barman there. Left together, drove home through Lowertown, turned right, took the short cut by the creamery and over Hunts Hill and stopped there on the brow as the full moon was out and then home. Went straight to bed. Don't know if the girls were here or stayed the night."

> 3
>
> Regarding December 23rd between waking up and the call from Eddie Cassidy
>
> "Awake at 8 a.m. - 9a.m. on Monday 23.12.1996, got up and made coffee. Jules in bed. Returned to bed with coffee. Tuned into Gaelic. Got up again at 10a.m. Was going to go to Skibbereen in the early afternoon, but Cassidy's phone call changed that so I was just "pottering" around until that."

> 4
>
> Regarding December 23rd from Eddie Cassidy's call through to 4pm

> "Eddie Cassidy contacted me about murder, asked me where it was and I was able to tell him exactly as I knew Alfie Lyons because I was helping him to do his garden and in the Spring of 1996 or 1995 the French lady arrived with her son and one other. Doing the garden for a few days over a 3 week period. Never spoke to her.
>
> Cassidy rang at 2p.m. on the Monday and I went to the scene with Jules. Stayed not too long. Stopped off at Post Office at Toormore and spoke to the Post Mistress. Checked phone book and got her name, listed there as Buinoil. Papers - Examiner 1st.
>
> Back to scene with Mike Brown, freelance photographer, at about 4p.m. and Eddie Cassidy."

Bailey embellishes his stories in several statements and goes into more detail than normal. The large amount of detail he gives when explaining why he chose to go to Dreenane is an excellent example. It is illuminating to read his reasons for going there while keeping in mind that in a few years, he will say he did not know where to go and ended up in Dreenane by happenstance. A further curiosity is that his tale about working for Lyons in the summer of 1995 does not in the slightest explain why he opted to go there. It is the victory of form over substance, and when it comes to murder, substance is what is needed. This is the behaviour of a man who should have never been believed without corroboration.

The deceased

Ian Bailey knew the people who lived in the house closest to the deceased person. Strange then he drove straight to the crime scene without first checking with his friends if AGS were in situ. To drive to such an obscure place without checking is an unusual course of action. It was as if he was certain the dead woman would be there.

The location of the cottages was and is very important. They were out in the open countryside, remote, and well-hidden. A person driving there would have to get onto the Dunmanus-Toormore road and look out for an unsigned turn-off onto an essentially single-track lane, hardly a road. When driving down the track, the cottages remain invisible for approximately 1000 metres. The lane comes to a dead end when the cottages are reached. The lane does not lead anywhere else.

The red flag for any investigative officer was, how did Bailey know where to find the dead body? His knowing would immediately make him become a person of significant interest. There appears to be no one else who knew with certainty where to find the deceased. Bailey could have said so without naming his source if someone other than Cassidy had told him the location.

He claimed that he had seen Sophie only once before she died. That was in the summer of 1995. He had been doing some labouring work for her neighbours, Alfie Lyons and Shirley Foster. They were friends of Bailey. He said he had seen Sophie in the distance and insisted he never saw her at close quarters nor spoke to her. Bailey said he knew it was the woman's holiday home and that she was French. Lyons says he introduced Sophie to Bailey. This was denied by Bailey.

Yet Bailey says he knew exactly where to go when he had spoken to Eddie Cassidy and he set off for Dreenane in a matter of minutes. There are important unanswered questions that Bailey would have been asked in a trial. He would have to explain how he knew Sophie still owned the cottage. Either he spoke to people very close to the time of the murder who confirmed she was still the owner, or he knew from her. Neither Bailey nor anyone else has confirmed the former.

Even if Bailey knew she still owned the cottage, how did he know she was there two days before Christmas? There was every chance she would be in France preparing for family celebrations. Sometimes, Sophie let her friends use the cottage while she stayed in France. If that were the case, how was Bailey certain that the victim was Sophie rather than one of her friends? Furthermore, how could Bailey know the nationality of the friend?

If those questions were not enough, at least one more is significant. How could Bailey know Sophie was there alone? More often than not, she went to the cottage with others. This time she travelled alone, having been unable to find a travelling companion. We have a situation where Bailey does not ask Cassidy about the victim and the other potential occupants. When he meets Sophie's neighbour, Shirley Foster, he does not ask her about the dead woman and who is staying at the cottage. Finally, he does not ask the officers any questions about the other occupants of the cottage. They would not have answered, but Bailey asked nothing, so he learned nothing. In the absence of knowing who was staying at the cottage, how did Bailey know that the deceased person was Sophie and not one of her guests? These are all questions he failed to answer but he would have been required to answer them at a trial.

One more issue regarding Bailey. After speaking to Eddie Cassidy, he did not call Lyons or Foster. He knew they were Sophie's neighbours.. A quick call to them would not only have confirmed that Dreenane was the scene of the crime, but it would have allowed Bailey to check whether the cottage was Sophie's, check whether she was there, and if there who else was staying there. Based on his actions and comments, he did not have the answers to these important questions, and he did nothing to get them. He was either the worst and least interested journalist ever, or he knew the answers already.

Furthermore, while in Dreenane, Bailey not only fails to ask Foster any questions, he fails to visit his friend Alfie Lyons. There is also no record of Bailey contacting Foster and Lyons later that day.

All his actions that day suggest he knew that the victim was Sophie, who had been alone at the cottage

Further indications of Bailey's culpability

As further statements were collected, there were many more reasons to doubt Bailey's version of events. The more that was learned about his statement the more it became a reasonable conclusion that he deliberately sought to hide the truth. For this chapter, a few key points will be emphasised. Each one is a significant piece of circumstantial evidence that points to Bailey's guilt. When combined, they readily make Bailey the prime suspect.

More lies in the 31.12.1996 statement: Box 1

In the statement, Bailey says that the top of the tree was cut down on Sunday morning. This was consistent with his insistence that he stayed at the Prairie on the night of December 21st. This becomes a problem because he lied about where he was, late on the 21st and early on the 22nd. He did not stay at home. He went to Schull and drank heavily, and stayed there until around lunchtime on the 22nd. Once Bailey admitted that he stayed at the Murphy home, he was caught in other lies. If he was in Schull on the 22nd until lunchtime then he lied about cutting down the tree that morning. When people lie prolifically, they struggle to keep up with their own dishonesty.

The false alibi: Box 2 and in part Box 3

This was devastating for Bailey's case. He said he got home, went to bed, and did not get up until sometime between 8 am and 9 am on the morning of the 23rd. His statement was corroborated by his partner Jules Thomas. At the time Sophie was being murdered, Bailey appeared to have an alibi. He was asleep in bed with Thomas. However, AGS was being given evidence suggesting that Bailey had provided a false alibi. On 10.02.1997, Bailey and Thomas were arrested and questioned. Thomas almost immediately confirmed that she had misinformed AGS and explained she could not account for where he was that night. this lent support to the suggestion he was elsewhere. After initially sticking with his December 31st story, Bailey capitulated. Despite his weasel words he was admitting he had given officers a false alibi. He had lied to officers trying to catch a brutal murderer. Why would an innocent man behave this way, and why did he never offer a meaningful explanation for his false alibi?

Bailey was severely incriminating himself. He was caught in several lies. Most notably, he had given a false alibi to AGS and knew where to find the body when he had no reason to do so.

A moment of reflection

Let's pause for a moment. Imagine you are investigating this murder. One man lies to officers where he was the night and morning before the murder. He says he knew the exact location of the deceased. This was despite it being in an obscure setting and Bailey not bothering to check it was the right place to go. Finally, he gave the police a false alibi. What would you think? When describing his arrest, Bailey said he could not understand why he had been arrested. To most people, it was obvious.

It did not stop there. As we will see, Ian Bailey was the person who most often contradicted Ian Bailey. For decades, he would come up with new stories that contradicted what he had once said. With time, he would often contradict those newer stories. It was lying on an industrial scale. All these lies were about the case and seeking to distance himself from what he had done.

Lies, contradictions, and more lies - the significant changes made by Bailey regarding his actions between 1 am and 1.40 pm on December 23rd, 1996

Ian Bailey claimed he made some slight errors in his statements to AGS. The DPP concurred with this. The supporters of Bailey blindly regurgitate this point of view, apparently oblivious to the actual details. Later, in the 2019 trial in France, the prosecution argued that he had made many changes in substance. If they were correct, then Bailey had repeatedly lied, and he could not be trusted with anything he said. That, all claims by Bailey needed to be thoroughly corroborated by others if they were to be given any credence.

So, let's take a look at the evidence. Not the spin or the empty opinions of the ignorant. We will look at the statements made by Ian Bailey on three important occasions. His lengthy statement on 31.12.1996. this has been the focus of this chapter so far. It showed us Bailey had guilty knowledge – the whereabouts of the deceased - and lied to the Garda. The second was the statements made by Bailey when under arrest on 10.02.1997. The third set of statements was made during his second arrest on 27.01.1998. in all cases, a written record was made and Bailey signed off those statements.

A sharp contrast

Before looking at what Bailey told AGS in detail, it will be helpful to compare what he told them on 31.12.1996 and his final version given on the evening of 27.01.1998, thirteen months later. Amazingly Bailey appears to be describing two completely different events. Not a single detail in his 1996 version is present thirteen months later.

It is difficult to understand how any sane person could conclude that Bailey did not change his statements. There can be no doubt that the story was changed. In Part Three, it will be shown that the DPP could read the statements below and conclude that nothing changed.

Original Version 31.12.1996	Final version 27.01.1998 20.02
Awake at 8a.m. - 9a.m. on Monday 23.12.1996, got up and made coffee. Jules in bed. Returned to bed with coffee. Tuned into Gaelic. Got up again at 10a.m. Was going to go to Skibbereen in the early afternoon, but Cassidy's phone call changed that so I was just "pottering" around until that. ALL THIS HAS GONE in 1998	I did not lie to you - we didn't have the right story. I went to bed about 1.30 a.m. - 2 a.m. Up at 4 a.m. to write - 30/35 minutes writing - then back to bed. Got up at 9 a.m. and went down to Studio to finish the article. NONE OF THIS WAS SAID IN DECEMBER 1996

How Bailey made himself the prime suspect from the beginning

The information provided in the statements made it clear that Bailey was trying to mislead the Police. A closer look at the changes made from statement to statement demonstrates the many changes Bailey made. He made at least twenty changes to his narrative. The changes are itemised below:

Statements made by Ian Bailey

> x20xxx   31.12.96
>
> Awake at 8a.m. - 9a.m. on Monday 23.12.1996, got up and made coffee. Jules in bed. Returned to bed with coffee. Tuned into Gaelic. Got up again at 10a.m. Was going to go to Skibbereen in the early afternoon, but Cassidy's phone call changed that so I was just "pottering" around until that.

> x21xxx   10.02.97   09.40
>
> Got up early, made coffee for Jules and brought it to bed. It was about 9.30a.m.-10a.m. went back to bed listened to the Radio. Spoke about what had to be done and we were going to Skibbereen, Co. Cork together, to deliver a turkey and do some shopping.
>
> Now 8am to 9am becomes 9.30am to 10am. Substantial change in the time. (1)

x23 xxxx   10.02.97   17.30

Q. Did you leave the house after going home with Jules?

A. I went to bed, I stayed in bed all night until next morning, I never left the house that night, Jules will tell ye.

Bailey is adamant that he stayed in bed until the following morning and never left the house.

x24 xxx   10.02.97   No time

It was then put to him that Jules stated that he left the bed and returned the following morning with a mark on his forehead.

He denied this.

I put it to him that he left the house.

He replied - We got home between one and two o'clock and went to bed.

Sometime after going to bed I got up - Did a bit of writing - the kitchen. I then went down to the studio I am not sure what time it was but it was dark. I have no watch. I had a story to write for Tribune and was told it was okay that Tuesday would do. It was a story about the Internet. I went back to Jules house at about 11a.m.

He did get up in the night (2)

He was in the kitchen (3)

He did some writing (4)

He went to the studio (5)

He mentions the Tribune (6)

He returned to the house at about 11am (7)

No making coffee (8)

No return to bed (9)

No listening to the radio (10)

No planning the day with Jules Thomas (11)

No pottering around (12)

And now the alibi collapses. Elsewhere Thomas had withdrawn her assertion that Bailey was in bed all night through to the morning and all that coffee making and radio listening.

x25 xxxx   10.02.97   No time

You have told us several times on this day that you went home from the Galley pub with Jules, then went to bed and did not get up until the following morning. Now you have told the other officer that you in fact did get up that night and left Jules house. Yes I now remember that I did get up and go to my studio. (Rented house) to do some work.

Why are you now changing your story regarding that night, is it because you are aware that Jules is now saying that you did get up.

No, "I remember now".

He had not said in the past that he had forgotten and NOW he remembered. He was giving completely different 'memories' in previous versions. Bailey is flapping around trying to offer a new version. This changing of his alibi illustrates his desperation.

x27 xxxx   27.01.98   12.25

Q.Tell us exactly what is the position in relation to the night of the 22nd/23rd December, 1996 when you arrived home with Jules ?

A. We just went to bed.

Q. Did you stay in bed ?

A Well no I got out of bed o.k.

Q .Where did you go ?

A.I went into the kitchen and did some writing.

Q. Did you leave the house ?

A. I did go to my studio in the morning by this I mean 9 a.m roughly, I had an article to write for the Tribune. It was due to be in on Monday 23rd December it concerned the intro of internet in West Cork. I had arranged with Tom McSweeney to have the copy of my report delivered to the Tribune before lunch on the 23rd December. I rang Mr. Bob Curran, Business Editor Tribune around 10 a.m. - 10.30 a.m. on Monday and he said that the article didn't have to be in until Tuesday.

He went to the studio at 9am (13)

9am was not in darkness (14)

New details added regarding Tribune contacts (got name wrong) (15)

Specific time given re calling Tribune *1 (16)

*1 Tribune deny any call in from Bailey

---

x32 xxxx   27.01.98   signed 20.02

Discussed movement of himself and Jules on Sunday 22/23/12/96.

Lied to police in his original questionnaire and statement.

I did not lie to you - we didn't have the right story.

I went to bed about 1.30 a.m. - 2 a.m. Up at 4 a.m. to write - 30/35 minutes writing - then back to bed. Got up at 9 a.m. and went down to Studio to finish the article.

Later time for going to bed with Jules Thomas (17)

Specific time regarding getting up (18)

Specific time about working in the kitchen (19)

Now able to give timings having said he did not have a watch (20)

What on earth does Bailey mean when he says "I did not lie to you - we didn't have the right story"? This is another slip by Bailey. He switches, within a sentence from I to we. What is the right story? And why were 'they' previously telling the wrong story (stories)?

The facts tell us that Bailey wanted us and would have wanted a Jury. to believe that when he gave his statement on 31.12.1996 he had forgotten that he got up in the night and went to the kitchen and did some writing for an article he was due to submit on the 23rd. He wanted people to believe he had forgotten all about going to the Studio to work for several hours, and while there, he made a phone call to the Tribune newspaper. Bailey also expected people to believe that all the following things he said to be true on 31.12.1996 were false memories rather than bare-faced lies. These included: he slept through the night, got up and made coffee, returned to bed, listened to the radio, made plans with Jules Thomas, and finally, pottered around for the morning. Which sane person could believe these were all false memories rather than deliberate lies?

This is preposterous. The DPP claiming Bailey did not change his story was nonsensical. The evidence is incontrovertible. Here, it is not a case of who to believe. We are not being asked whether we believe Bailey or the many people who flatly contradict him, more of that later. He is regularly contradicting himself. Bailey cannot be believed at all. He continuously lies and changes his story. As it is obvious that Bailey kept lying, one is justified in asking why he had done so and what inferences can one reasonably make. In the DPP report that prevented a trial for Bailey, it was stated:

> "The fact that Bailey and Jules Thomas have made errors in their recollection does not necessarily mean they are deliberately lying. Errors made by other persons are regarded as simple mistakes in terms of recollection."

In part three of this book, it becomes apparent that the DPP did not do a detailed analysis of all Bailey's statements. A reference to 'have made errors' is not good enough. There is no calculation regarding the number of these 'errors,' nor are there any qualitative insights. An error such as saying it was tea, not coffee, or naming the wrong radio station Bailey listened to is significantly different from giving a false alibi.

Ian Bailey's initial version of events was presented at the beginning of this chapter. The notes below are the version he presented thirteen months later. It was a completely different story. The first version presented a profoundly dishonest narrative, plus a few truths that were corroborated by others. These truths exposed his culpability. By 1998, the version left out those truths. Those who once corroborated Bailey's few honest statements now contradicted his new false narratives.

There is one further important observation to be made about the statements of Bailey and Jules Thomas regarding their activities on the morning and early afternoon of December 23rd, 1996. This is concerning the time between getting up that day and the phone call from Eddie Cassidy. It is not what they said about their activities between 8 am and 1.40 pm, a period of almost six hours, it was what they did not say. On the day that Sophie is murdered, Bailey begins by offering a false alibi and then a 'black hole' in which he essentially makes coffee and then 'potters about' until 1.40 pm. In subsequent statements, Bailey concocts a variety of narratives which include him doing some writing. Even these variations on a theme tend to stop around 11 am. Jules Thomas is equally reticent about her activities at that time.

In chapter three we will see that according to more than ten reliable witnesses including Fenella and Saffron Thomas, Bailey and Jules Thomas were very active between 8 am and 1.40 pm. However, they were activities not found in their statements. During that period, they were reported to have done and said things that pointed to Ian Bailey's guilt. Fortunately, the collection of hundreds of timeline statements from people, something Bailey probably did not anticipate, enabled investigators to discover what people were doing even when they themselves failed to declare certain actions in their statements. An example of this was the way Bailey's lies about where he was the night of the 21st and the morning of the 22nd were exposed due to the statements of the Murphys and others staying at the Murphy home on that evening.

Ian Bailey's omissions helped hide his guilty behaviour for decades. The DPP appears to have believed them. In chapter three, the truth will be presented, and the reasons why Bailey was so evasive will be understood.

The whole of this chapter is about Bailey lying. It is not whether we believe Bailey versus others but whether, given his repeated self-contradictions, we can believe anything he says. The view in this book is that without reliable corroboration, it would be foolish to take his word alone. He could not be trusted.

The next two chapters will show how dozens of individual timelines show how Bailey lied about the events of the 23rd and how he continued to trap himself.

For statements, see Appendix 2: pt 1 pt 2 pt 3

Notes

Bailey's 1998 version of what happened the night Sophie Toscan du Plantier was murdered

On the evening of December 21st and the morning of the 22nd

In 1998, Bailey was now telling AGS investigators that on the evening and night of the 21st, he was drinking in Schull through to the early hours of the 22nd. He slept at the Ardamanagh Road home of Patricia Murphy. There were several adults staying there that night.

He remained in Schull until sometime between noon and 1 p.m. While there, he bought newspapers and later got a lift home.

When he arrived home, Jules was not there. He now says it was early afternoon when he alone killed the turkeys and later cut down the tree with Saffron. It was in 1997-8 that Bailey eventually claimed he got some scratches.

The initial story was about a few cuts from the bow saw. By 1997, this blossomed into stories of scratches from turkeys and from pulling the cut-down tree.

The evening of the 22nd

By 1998, Bailey had completely changed his story about the journey home. In the later version, the couple left the Galley bar. They had been there several hours before returning home. While there, Bailey danced around while playing on his drum.

Bailey, for no apparent reason, took a far longer route home after leaving the bar. He stopped the car on Hunt's Hill, got out, and looked across the valley. He could see the few detached cottages that were in Dreenane. A few hours later, it would be the scene of Sophie's murder.

The morning of the 23rd

In the 1998 version, Bailey no longer sleeps alongside Jules Thomas from 1 am to 9 am. At some point, he gets up and goes to the kitchen to work on an article with an imminent deadline. He works on it for approximately 30 minutes. He then goes back to bed and sleeps there until 9 am. He suggests he is asleep at the time Sophie is murdered, but no one can confirm it. At 9 am he gets up and walks to the Studio, which is 200 metres away. While there he says he telephoned the Tribune newspaper and got an extension to December 24th for the article. He does not say who he spoke to nor explain the reason he needed the extension nor the reason he needed an extension to the 24th rather than until the end of the 23rd. He made no mention of the new extension time.

The call and the following eighty minutes

Ian Bailey says he was either told the deceased person was a non-national, or a non-national, possibly French.

He did not know where to find the crime scene. Bailey and Thomas jumped in their car and set off, driving without a destination in mind. For an unknown reason, they somehow found themselves driving south on the Dunmanus – Toormore Road. Bailey never explained why as an experienced journalist he took to driving along small roads in remote countryside.

At the junction between that road and Dreenane Lane, by happenstance, they met up with Shirley Foster. It is this 'chance' meeting that leads to Bailey being directed to the scene of the crime. (not his claim of knowing exactly where to go)

After a brief exchange with the Police officers, Bailey then drove to the Post office. He made no comment on why he chose that course of action. This time, he arrived there with no idea who the victim might be. When there, there was a second case of happenstance when the Post Mistress told him about the murder and gave Bailey the victim's name without being asked anything. This version of the Post office visit had zero corroboration and was contradicted by all other parties

CHAPTER 3

Two contradictory narratives: Both cannot be true

> Regarding December 23rd, 1996
>
> "...after that I spoke with my Mum possibly 11 or 12 to ask her for a lift........she said on the phone there had been a murder "
>
> Saffron Thomas statement

If the above statement by Saffron Thomas is corroborated and believed, then Ian Bailey and Jules Thomas have lied to everyone, including what they told AGS about when they first knew about the murder. It raises serious questions about what they were trying to cover up.

Ian Bailey and Jules Thomas have repeatedly stated that the first time they knew about the death of a woman in the Toormore area was at 1.40 pm. This resulted from a telephone call from Cork Examiner journalist Eddie Cassidy. In his original Police statement made on 31.12.1996, Bailey stated that when Cassidy gave him a general description of the location of the body, he said, "Eddie Cassidy contacted me about murder, asked me where it was, and I was able to tell him exactly as I knew Alfie Lyons because I was helping him to do his garden and in the Spring of 1996 or 1995 the French lady arrived with her son and one other." Both he and Thomas made a beeline for three cottages in Dreenane. This was confirmed by Shirley Foster, who met them on Dreenane Lane.

The question has always been how they could immediately know the victim lived in this remote location. The simplest explanation was that they knew where to go because Bailey had murdered the woman.

Saffron Thomas

On the 12th of October 2011, Saffron Thomas, the eldest daughter of Jules Thomas, was interviewed by French investigators concerning the murder of Sophie Toscan du Plantier. The interview was video recorded, and Thomas confirmed and signed the written record. She had made a similar statement nine years earlier. Her statement makes it clear that Jules Thomas and, by extension, Ian Bailey knew about the murder many hours before the time they gave to the Police. This leaves important questions unanswered. How did they know so soon? Why did they give AGS a false time?

In her interview, Saffron Thomas described her activities on the morning of 23.12.1996. She says she had stayed overnight on the 22nd at a friend's home in Schull. Later the next morning, she walked into the town centre where she had a coffee. Her statement is found at the beginning of this chapter. Between 11 and 12, Jules Thomas told her daughter there had been a murder..

On its own, it would be a case of who to believe: Saffron or Bailey and Jules Thomas. However, this statement does not stand in isolation. It fits perfectly with statements taken from various other people, including journalists and Fenella Thomas. Based on these statements, it is possible to map out the truth.

What the statements tell us

The narrative is straightforward. Bailey says he was at home in the morning, but the only person who could have corroborated that—Fenella Thomas—contradicts it. Statements from Tribune journalists contradict Bailey's claim that he was speaking to the Tribune newspaper that morning. They tried calling him, but no one answered.

James Camier says that on the morning of the 23rd, Jules Thomas told him that Bailey had gone to the crime scene in Dreenane. Dick Cross and Michael McSweeney, experienced newspapermen, both say that Bailey told them he was at the crime scene that morning long before lunchtime. The times indicated by Cross, McSweeney, and Camier all match. This is compelling evidence. The suggestion that AGS officers, Camier, and two journalists conspired on this issue is preposterous. Nor should we forget that it is indirectly supported by Fenella Thomas, who said Bailey and J Thomas left home between 10 and 12. While

Bill Fuller observed Jules Thomas, alone, driving towards town at around 11 am. The timing here fits with that given by James Camier. Fuller also supports the view that Bailey had gone elsewhere and was not with Jules. In a statement Thomas confirmed she was shopping at that time. All these timings are consistent with the statement made by Saffron Thomas.

Ian Bailey claimed to have telephoned the Tribune around 10.30 am and stated he was given an extension for the article he was due to submit by 12 pm that day. Both the journalists who may have been able to grant an extension to Bailey say they had no contact with him until 4 pm to 5pm. Moreover, neither of them granted any type of extension. In their statements, they report trying to contact Bailey to find out what was happening but got no reply, and considering what they would do if the article were not submitted. If one believes Bailey, the journalists either lied and fabricated a whole story, or they had some sort of collective memory malfunction. If the journalists are being truthful, then Bailey lied in his statement. Once again, there is a choice between the pathological liar seeking to cover up his involvement in a murder versus two people recounting what happened while having no reason to lie nor antipathy directed towards Bailey.

Late that morning to noon two further witnesses spoke to Ian Bailey on the telephone when he called their home. He spoke to Paul O'Colmain and Caroline Leftwick. In both cases, Bailey told them he was busy working as a journalist on the case of a French woman murdered in the Toormore area. They reported that he seemed to be excited. Both Camier and Saffron Thomas are clear that Jules Thomas told them about the murder between 11 and 12. Caroline Leftwick and Paul O'Colmain both say Ian Bailey told them about the murder between 11 am and 12.30 pm. These are 4 independent reports of Bailey and J Thomas knowing about the murder long before Eddie Cassidy spoke to Bailey.

There is a further sighting of Bailey and Thomas together that morning by a neighbour, Donal O'Sullivan. He knew Bailey and Thomas and the car they drove, a Fiesta. He often 'met them on the Schull to Goleen road. The sighting took place around 12.20 to 12.30 pm on the 23rd. It stood out in O'Sullivan's mind because he saw them on a coastal road. This is further evidence that Bailey and Thomas were out and about on the morning of December 23rd, 1996.

Here is a full summary of the statements

Table of events

Time	Key points	Source
Approx. 10 am	Bailey and Jules Thomas are away from home for approximately 2 hrs	F Thomas
Pre 10.38 am	Bailey at the scene of the crime taking pictures before it was cordoned off	Dick Cross

	[Bailey proffers 2 contradictory stories about Monday morning 1. Pottering about 2. Working on an article for the Tribune. Bailey says he spoke to the Tribune to get an extension.	Ian Bailey
	Fenella says he was not there	F Thomas
	Two senior journalists at the Tribune say they heard nothing from Bailey until approximately 16.00 to 17.00. They did not receive a call from Bailey nor grant an extension. T McEnaney tried phoning Bailey but got no reply.	R Curran T McEnaney
11.00 am	Jules Thomas driving alone near the causeway	Bill Fuller
11.00- 11.30 am	Jules Thomas tells Camier a French woman is dead in Dreenane, and Bailey is there	James Camier
	Jules Thomas later confirms she saw the Camiers on Monday	J Thomas

Two contradictory narratives: Both cannot be true   51

10.30-11.00 am	Bailey tells Michael McSweeney he took photos of the scene of the crime between 10.30-and 11.00 am	M McSweeney
11.00-11.30 am	Bailey calls Paul O'Colmain and tells him about the local murder of a French woman	P O'Colmain
11.30-12.30	Bailey tells Caroline Leftwick their meeting is cancelled because he needs to work on the murder case	C Leftwick
Approx. 12.00	Jules Thomas tells Saffron about the murder	S Thomas
Approx 12.20/30	Bailey and J Thomas are seen out in their car.	D. O'Sullivan

If Bailey is to be believed, then every single alternative source listed must be lying, including Jules Thomas. Furthermore, the lies would have to be fully coordinated by people who did not know each other. For example, Camier says Jules told them that Bailey was in Dreenane checking out the murder. Meanwhile, Cross and McSweeney say Bailey told each of them independently that he had been to the Dreenane scene of the crime in the late morning. James Camier, Saffron Thomas, Caroline Leftwick, and Paul O'Colmain all say that within approximately an hour, they were told of the death of a French woman. Does anyone, other than Bailey and someone at the DPP, believe this is some strange coincidental and communal false memory? Or that it may be some huge conspiracy?

The table below summarises what Bailey and Thomas told six witnesses about events at Dreenane. There is a high level of consistency in what people are told.

	Time	Nationality	Cause of death	Location
Bailey told Cross	Around 2 pm said was there pre 11 am			Scene of the crime
Bailey told McSweeney	Around 2 pm said was there pre 11 am			Scene of the crime
Thomas told Camier	At 11 am to 11.30 am	French	Murdered	Dreenane
J Thomas to Saffron	Around Noon	French	Murdered	Unnamed but JT knew the location
Bailey to O'Colmain	11 am to 11.30 am	French	Murdered	Mentioned location but Does not recall name
Bailey to Leftwick	11.30 an to 12.30 pm	French	Murdered	Toormore

There are the ever-changing uncorroborated narratives pushed by Ian Bailey, occasionally aided by Thomas. The alternative set of statements that corroborate each other show Bailey had guilty knowledge of a French woman murdered in Dreenane. He had this knowledge long before he claims he learned about the incident.

There are two mutually exclusive narratives. When one is accepted, the other must be treated as a tissue of lies. The conclusion must be that all those witnesses are not lying and Bailey in particular, is highly culpable,

The implications of what Saffron Thomas and others tell us

Shirley Foster discovered the body of the victim at around 10 am on the 23rd of December. The Police arrived at 10.38 am While the circumstances were brutal and suspicious, there could be no conclusion that a murder had taken place for many hours. Fenella Thomas stated that Bailey and Thomas left the cottage between 9 am and 10 am so they left before the body was found.

How would Bailey and Thomas have so much information about the crime for all these calls and conversations if they knew nothing until 13.40 pm that day? How could they know so many details when they had left the cottage before the dead body of Sophie had been discovered?

A wide variety of people provided a coherent narrative. They did not know each other. They told investigators that Bailey and Thomas knew that a French woman was dead, actually murdered, and she could be found in Dreenane. How could this be known? This means Bailey and Thomas knew about the murder of a French woman at least 3.5 hours earlier than they had said. The indications are they knew before Shirley Foster. If Bailey had been given that information before 10 am by a third party, he would have mentioned it in his journalism. He did not.

If they knew all this, there is every chance that they would know the victim's identity. If a single witness states this information regarding either Bailey or Thomas, it might be possible to question its veracity. In this case, several people in various situations are telling a story that fits together.

If all the other statements were unknown, leaving only that of Saffron Thomas in 2011, it would be a hammer blow for Ian Bailey and reveal shocking behaviour by Jules Thomas. However, six witnesses directly heard comments from Bailey and J Thomas showing they knew about the murder early morning on 23.12.1996

> The independent evidence from 6 people that Ian Bailey and Jules Thomas had detailed knowledge of the murder many hours before the call from Eddie Cassidy.
>
> **Ian Bailey**
>
> Comments to Dick Cross, Michael McSweeney, Paul O'Colmain and Caroline Leftwick.
>
> **Jules Thomas**
>
> Comments to Mr Camier and Saffron Thomas

> With supportive statements from Fenella Thomas, Bill Fuller, Richard Curran, Tom McEnaney, Donal O'Sullivan and Jules Thomas

The DPP knew all this corroborating evidence when they refused to charge Bailey. There is an irrefutable case that Ian Bailey and Jules Thomas knew about the murder very early on 23.12.1996. One that should have been tested in court.

Three scenarios of the period 8 am to 1.40 pm on December 23rd, 1996

In Chapter 2, the constantly changing story of Ian Bailey between 1996 and 1998 was presented. It shows how it is impossible to believe his statements and evidence. Given his incessant dishonesty, most people would not take anything Bailey said at face value. It was Bailey himself who was destroying his credibility and plausibility. In this chapter, we learned why he was lying. One can see the things he was seeking to hide. These include the very early knowledge of the murder, where it happened, and the identity of the victim.

In the table below are the relevant parts of the signed statements provided by Ian Bailey in 1996 and 1998 for the time between 8 am and 1.40 pm. A detailed analysis of his statements in Chapter 2 showed that he made at least twenty factual changes in his accounts of what he did on 23.12.1996. In the totality of his signed statements for the morning and early afternoon of the 23rd, there is little more than falsehoods, contradictions, plus no corroboration. This is evident in columns 1 and 2 of the table.

In the third column of the table, the narrative is provided by other witnesses. These people have several interactions with Bailey and Thomas, and it is abundantly clear that the pair were very active that morning, and their actions all showed they knew about the murder long before the 1.40 pm phone call.

Bailey 1996	Bailey 1998	Alternative narrative
	After at least twenty changes. Every one uncorroborated	At least 12 independent corroborative witnesses
Awake at 8a.m. - 9a.m. on Monday 23.12.1996, got up and made coffee. Jules in bed. Returned to bed with coffee. Tuned into Gaelic. Got up again at 10a.m. Was going to go to Skibbereen in the early afternoon, but Cassidy's phone call changed that so I was just "pottering" around until that.	I did not lie to you - we didn't have the right story.

I went to bed about 1.30 a.m. - 2 a.m. Up at 4 a.m. to write - 30/35 minutes writing - then back to bed. Got up at 9 a.m. and went down to Studio to finish the article.

[Says he made a call to the Tribune around 10.30] | Bailey and Thomas left the house between 09.00 and 10.00. Bailey went to / was dropped off in Dreenane. Bailey tells 2 journalists he was there that morning

He failed to hit his article deadline that lunchtime |

Two contradictory narratives: Both cannot be true 57

		Thomas is driving into Schull alone around 11.00 While there speaks to the Camiers telling them about the murder and Bailey being in the Dreenane area investigating it as a journalist
		Bailey makes calls to O'Colmain and Leftwick telling them both he is doing journalistic work 11.00-12.30
Nothing else until Cassidy called at 13,40	Nothing else until Cassidy called at 13,40	He and Thomas are out in the car around 12.00-12.30
		Saffron Thomas spoke to Jules on the phone around noon, and she was told about the murder.

In chapter two, we saw how Ian Bailey's ever-changing statements exposed him as a man trying to cover up his culpability for Sophie's murder. In this chapter, the evidence, including that from 3 members of the Thomas family and 4 reputable journalists, shows that Bailey and Thomas knew about the murder many hours before it became public and before the time they claimed they were informed of the death. Ian Bailey knew about the murder long before he received a call from Eddie Cassidy.

The findings described in chapters 2 and 3 present a liar with the knowledge that only the perpetrator or someone close to the perpetrator could possess. There is no indication that Bailey was informed by a third party. In chapter four, Bailey's further lies and the consistent evidence of others add considerable support to the conclusion that Bailey murdered Sophie Toscan du Plantier.

For statements, see Appendix 2: pt 4

CHAPTER **4**

80 minutes - Caught in a trap of his own making

In chapter two, the lies and contradictions of Ian Bailey were mapped out in terms of his early statements accounting for what he was doing over the Christmas weekend up to the telephone call at 1.40 pm received by Bailey at the Prairie on the 23rd of December 1996. In chapter three, statements of a dozen witnesses were combined to prove that Bailey knew about the murder in Dreenane long before his call from Eddie Cassidy and before the body was found.

This chapter focuses on an eighty-minute timeslot running from 1.40 p.m. to 3 p.m. on the same day. The pattern of lies and contradictions continues as before. Bailey's final narrative bears no resemblance to the original—there is no surprise there. The statements for this important period of time lend significant support to the conclusions in the earlier chapters.

First, he makes changes repeatedly between 1998 and the 2020s. He lies to explain a certain scenario, and when those lies create new contradictions, he lies again. Secondly, we begin with Bailey's original narrative, which several people corroborate. For once several people unrelated to

Bailey, plus Jules Thomas, support his early statements. In most cases, this is a good thing. However, the original story is damning. It shows Bailey had detailed knowledge about the crime and the victim that only the murderer, or someone close to the murderer, could possess. Bailey spends the next twenty-plus years changing his story to cover up this guilty knowledge. His problem is that everyone else who corroborated his original story makes no changes, and eventually, their statements go from corroborating Bailey to contradicting him.

If what Thomas and others have said for over 26 years was true, then Bailey had repeatedly given false evidence in an attempt to cover up his involvement in the murder. Given the extensive lying presented in Chapter 2, this is par for the course. Bailey's frequent self-contradictions highlight his dishonesty. In this chapter, other people contradict him. The most notable of these people was Jules Thomas. She stuck to her original narrative about these events. By doing so, she went from fully agreeing with Bailey to contradicting all his later narratives.

To accept what Bailey says from 1998 onwards necessitates that people must disbelieve Thomas. By accepting what Thomas stated, it cannot be denied that Bailey has lied. There is more to this choice. To agree with Bailey requires people to conclude that everyone else is lying or making exactly the same mistake as Thomas. In this scenario, everyone contradicts Bailey while agreeing with each other. Those who find Thomas more plausible will see that many others corroborate her story while only the ever-changing Bailey nay says it.

The original story told by Bailey and Thomas concerning their post 1.40 pm activities

In 1996 and 1997, in her statements and interview answers, Jules Thomas gave a clear timeline for what Ian Bailey said and did in the eighty minutes following a call from journalist Eddie Cassidy on December 23rd, 1996. At 1.40 pm, Bailey says he was asked to check out an incident involving a dead woman in Toormore.

The Schull resident and artist has consistently said Ian Bailey told her the dead woman in Toormore was French, and she and Bailey drove directly to Dreenane as he said he knew exactly where to find the body. They approached the crime scene on a narrow lane connecting the main road to the hidden cottages. Halfway along the lane, they met Shirley Foster, who was coming in the opposite direction. Although a journalist, Bailey did not bother asking Foster questions about the crime scene and what she may have observed or knew. The Gards at the scene told Bailey nothing about the crime or the victim. They said he should contact AGS communications department in Dublin for details. He then drove to the Toormore Post Office. Bailey said he wanted to find the name of the French woman who owned the cottage because she was the dead victim.

Several people independently corroborated this account. Photographic Editor Padraig Bierne said that when Bailey called him at 1.55 p.m., he told him the victim was French. Shirley Foster has given several statements describing her meeting with Bailey halfway down Dreenane Lane.

She explained that Bailey told her he was there on behalf of the press but asked no questions.

> **Shirley Foster 22.05.97**
>
> "I was on my own and as stated it was about 2.15/2.20p.m. on the 23.12.1996. As I drove out past the tape and on out towards the road intersections I met a car coming towards me and as the road is narrow I pulled in to allow it pass by. I saw it was Ian Baily and Jules Thomas. Ian Baily was driving. I am certain of that. I left down the window as did Ian did. I said words to the effect "The police have barriers there" and he said I am here on official business."

A statement made by Detective Garda Margaret Murrell explained how she and other officers, accompanied by Jules Thomas, drove to Dreenane. While there, Thomas showed them where she took photographs and the place where Bailey spoke to the Gards. The other thing Jules pointed out was the place where she and Bailey met Shirley Foster. It was not at the junction of Dunmanus-Toormore Road and Dreenane Lane, as Bailey latterly claimed. They met partway down Dreenane Lane. This is further confirmation that Bailey knew where he was going and he was driving directly to Sophie's cottage. It also highlights how Bailey completely changed his story at this pivotal point.

The Post Mistress and Post Office worker confirmed that Bailey had gone to the Post Office to get the name of the French owner of a cottage. The Post Office worker Ann Dukelow stated, 'He told me that it was the French woman in Dreenane that was killed. He asked me did I know her name and I said I did." The Post Mistress, Nan Jermyn, added that later, after leaving the Post Office, Bailey telephoned them to check the precise spelling of the Frenchwoman's surname. It was Bouniol.

This was the story told by Bailey in his 1996 and 1997 statements. His original version of events in 1996 and again in 1997 was in full agreement with Thomas. Not only does he say the victim was French, but we also know he said he knew 'exactly' where the body could be found. He said he had a brief conversation with Foster on Dreenane Lane and stated that when he went to the Post office, he "Checked phone book and got her name, listed there as Bouniol." There is considerable consistency in the reports on what Bailey said and did. However, these agreed facts became highly problematic for Ian Bailey. He had revealed several incriminating truths. In 1998 Bailey told a completely different story.

Bailey's problems

The original timeline portrays Ian Bailey as the investigative journalist who gets out there and digs up the facts. Look closer, and it shows something else. If the statements were true, it meant Ian Bailey knew for sure the dead woman was French; he knew where the body could be found, and he knew the dead woman was the owner of a cottage in Dreenane. Yet during that eighty minutes, no one had told him any of this. How could he know? For over 27 years, he has failed to explain how he knew these details.

As the statements stood in 1997, Bailey could not explain what he knew. In 1998 he changed his entire story, hoping no one would notice.

The 1998 version

Bailey said he knew exactly where to go when called by Eddie Cassidy. He confirmed that assertion by directly driving to Dreenane. In his 31st December statement, he even sought to explain why he knew where to go on the 23rd. He was probably quite pleased with his explanatory narrative. He says the victim was French; he knew a French woman who lived locally, and thus, he drove straight there. Job done. However, he was not as clever as he thought, and his nice little narrative started to fall apart. Eddie Cassidy insisted that he had not mentioned anything about the victim's nationality. In all his other calls, at and around the time he called Bailey, Cassidy did not mention the victim's nationality. Fenella Thomas, Jules Thomas's youngest daughter, strongly supports Cassidy's account of his conversation. She was with Bailey and Jules Thomas when the call came through from Cassidy. Fenella Thomas answered the phone. She recounted what Bailey had said after the call.

> "There's a woman dead nearby. I don't think her nationality was discussed, just woman dead, body found that's all, somewhere nearby in Schull.".

Just as Cassidy asserted, there was no mention of nationality or cause of death and a vague reference to location. A powerful case can be made that Cassidy and Fenella Thomas should be believed. This makes Bailey's early insistence that the victim was French even more incriminating.

When interviewed by AGS in 1998, Bailey first switched his story from the victim being French to the victim being a non-national, possibly French. Perhaps he hoped this would deflect investigators from his original tale.

It is worth noting here that the nationality he says Cassidy gave him is yet another issue where Bailey failed to be specific. In the table below, a selection of the on-the-record versions proffered by Bailey is listed. Initially, in 1996 and 1997, Bailey was certain he was told the deceased was French. Then, on the morning of January 27th, 1998, he dropped the French element altogether, saying the victim was a non-national. In under twelve hours, a third version was offered. This time, Bailey thought Cassidy 'may have' said French. This is a significant departure from the assertion that he was told it was a French national.

At the 2003 Civil trial, Bailey presented a fourth version. Under oath, he was now certain that he was told the victim was a non-national, possibly French. This then became the narrative he stuck to. Except for the time when he made no mention of Cassidy saying anything about nationality in an article he wrote for the September 2021 copy of the Big Issue. This matches the version Cassidy had always told. A month later, in a further Big Issue article, Bailey reverted to his non-national, possibly French narrative. In total, that is five variations. If one is true, then the other four are false.

Bailey, on the nationality of the deceased

Date	Nationality
1996	French
1997	French
1998	Non-national (9.45 am) Non-national, may have said French (8.02 pm)
2003 trial	Non-national possibly French
2021 September Big Issue	No nationality given
2021 October Big Issue	Non Irish possibly French
2023 Shattered Lives podcast Claimed to have found original notes	Non-national possibly French [he says he made a written note at the time]

In 1996 and 1997, Bailey insisted he had been told the victim was French; then, for 25 years, from 1998 to 2023, he never again claimed he was told the victim was definitely French. This is not some small oversight or understandable error. It is significant.

Once Bailey has moved from French to non-national, possibly French, he is forced to make other changes. Once the victim was not identified as French, there would be no reason for him to drive straight to Dreenane. This also made a complete mockery of his 31.12.1996 statement. If he was saying the victim was a foreign national, why tell his tale about working for Alfie Lyons in 1995 and seeing Frenchwoman Sophie in the distance? His lies kept catching him out.

Having jettisoned his 31.12.1996 falsehoods, he had to explain how he ended up in Dreenane. A linked problem was that Bailey Thomas and Foster mentioned meeting halfway down Dreenane Lane. This was problematic for Bailey because Dreenane Lane connects the main road to the Dreenane cottages. It is a dead end along that lane. If Bailey was on it that could be his only destination. How could he explain randomly looking for a dead foreign national and ending up driving directly to the scene of the crime?

This led to a fantasy scenario in which Bailey is driving 'aimlessly' down the Dunmanus—Toormore road. He no longer had an explanation for driving down that road, so his rationale was that he just happened to drive down that road for no particular reason. This despite saying in 31.12.1996 that he knew 'exactly' where to go! One lie begets another. He then claims to have met Foster, not halfway down Dreenane Lane, but at the junction of the Dreenane Lane and the Dunmanus -Toormore road. In this new scenario, he claims that Shirley Foster tells him that there is a crime scene at the end of Dreenane Lane. This is Bailey's new explanation for how he learned about the crime scene. Foster allegedly points him in the direction of Dreenane without mentioning anything else about the crime including that she found the body. And Bailey asked no questions. Bailey kept digging deeper holes with his lies. This is a further dramatic change in his story. How could he claim he knew exactly where to go in his 1996 statement and then claim it was a stroke of luck that he bumped into Foster in his 1998 version?

Later, in 2011, when interviewed by French investigators, Foster voiced her anger at Bailey for replacing facts with his fiction.

"Subsequently, he lied about it. Later, he said that he had met me at the intersection when in reality, we crossed each other halfway between the intersection and the house, at the bend."

This radical shift needed us all to forget everything Bailey originally said about that eighty minutes on the 23rd. Bailey wanted people to dismiss the evidence that every other witness has stated and stuck to.

An example of Bailey changing his story

1996 and 1997 Bailey	1998 Bailey
"Eddie Cassidy contacted me about murder, asked me where it was and I was able to tell him exactly as I knew Alfie Lyons….i went to the scene with Jules" 1996 "On the road into Dreenane off the Dunmanus-Toormore Rd. we met Shirley Foster coming out in her car and I spoke to her. She said are you coming to visit and I said no that the paper had called me and asked us to go to the scene." 1997	"Bailey explained - Met Shirley at Junction of Dunmanus Road / Toormore Rd. and Dreenane Road. Asked her if there were any Guards about, she pointed back in the road. I didn't ask her anything about the murder or the scene." 1998

Bailey needed to make one final change. In 1996-97 he had gone to the Post Office to get the name of the French woman who owned the cottage at the crime scene. He must have realised that he could only go with that intention if he were sure the victim was Sophie. He wanted to hide his knowledge of the victim, so he needed to make further changes in his story. In 1998 he says he drove to the Post Office with no specific intention. Once there, he claimed that other people had spontaneously told him the victim's name. There can be only one reason Bailey made this change. The original version implicated him. Slowly he realised he had revealed he knew far too much about the deceased. In 1996, Bailey travelled to different places with specific intentions. By 1998, he was aimlessly driving around and bumping into people who disclosed vital pieces of information. He thought we might not notice, but we did.

Continued changes made by Bailey

Eighteen years after the murder, in 2014, Ian Bailey was still changing and embellishing his story. Regarding where he went on leaving the Prairie cottage after the Cassidy call, he sought to explain why he was driving down the Dunmanus-Toormore road. This was part of the cover-up of him driving directly to Dreenane. For this reason, he claimed he crossed paths with Foster while on the way to the Post Office! He had not referred to this Post office variation in eighteen years. Thomas has never mentioned it. This is just one further elaboration and distraction made by Bailey. It is as if an idea popped into the head of this pathological liar, so he says it. He thought people were gullible. He was wrong.

It is also evident he forgot that anyone travelling from the Prairie to the Post Office would not take the route he had selected. Something Sophie's uncle, Jean Pierre Gazeau, pointed out in the Irish Times in December 2022. In the 2003 libel case, Bailey had flipped back to his original assertion that he went straight to Dreenane. Eleven years later, in 2014, and again under oath, Bailey changes his tale. Gazeau explained:

> "...at the case in Dublin in 2014, Mr Bailey suddenly introduces this element that he decided to go Jermyn's Post Office as the post-office would know what foreigners were living in the area, so he and Jules Thomas drove over by Sophie's house at Dreenane, just over the hill from Dunmanus Bay."
>
> "The only problem is the quickest way to the Post Office from the Prairie is to go straight down the R592, Durrus to Toormore road and turn east on the R591, Goleen to Schull road – not go west to Dunmanus and over by Dreenane – it makes no sense to go by Sophie's house to go the Post Office."

A five-minute journey becomes a ten-minute journey for no reason. This is all Bailey fiction. His big idea. He is trying to explain why the meeting with Foster had been at that junction. He could only admit to 'bumping into' Foster at the end of Dreenane Lane if he was en route to the Post

Office. This is a desperate clutching at straws by a man who ran out of excuses long ago.

Thomas has been consistent throughout. They went to Dreenane and met Foster on the lane. Foster agrees. Bailey is cut adrift with his fantasy story.

As late as 2023, Bailey made further significant changes in his story when he claimed in his podcast, "Nan Jermyn (the Post Mistress) said that she had heard of the death and knew the victim as Sophie Bouniol." He was putting words in the mouth of a dead woman.

Yet in her 2011 statement to the French investigators, Jules Thomas stated, "We then went to the Post Office in Toormore and asked the postwoman if she knew the name of the person who lived next door to Alfie Lyons." If we believe Thomas's evidence, it is hard not to conclude that Bailey is playing fast and loose with the truth again.

Jules Thomas, Shirley Foster, and all the others from 1996 and 1997 have made no changes in their stories. Indeed, as we have seen, Foster has voiced her unhappiness about Bailey's brazen relocation of their meeting on Dreenane Lane. The original true story implicates Ian Bailey. For decades, he tried to muddy the waters. He failed.

For almost twenty-seven years, Jules Thomas has consistently told us what happened in the eighty minutes between 1.40 pm and 3 pm on 23.12.1996. What she said has been corroborated by many other independent witnesses. If she and others are telling the truth, then Bailey has delivered falsehood after falsehood and done so to cover up what he knew about the murder.

Bailey's 1996 and 1997 versions were corroborated by Jules Thomas, Padraig Bierne, Shirley Foster, 2 gards, Ann Dukelow, and Nan Jermyn. His post-1997 versions were corroborated by no one and contradicted by everyone.

Ian Bailey did not have to prove his innocence, but he would have been required to explain the repeated changes in his story. He would have had to explain why he repeatedly contradicted himself. He would be called to account for his falsehoods and lies. He would have been compelled to explain what motivated the huge changes between 1996 and 1998. High on the list of explanations sought would be why he told AGS he knew exactly where to find the crime scene (in 1996) but, in later years, offered a convoluted tale of taking the slow route to the post office and bumping into Foster at a junction.

The changes made by Bailey were not random. They were systematic and linked to him seeking to hide his original and fully corroborated narrative. A narrative that implicated him in Sophie's murder.

Throughout this book, Bailey's frequent lies are exposed. The few things he said that were corroborated by Jules Thomas were soon jettisoned when they both changed their stories. In the case of the eighty minutes, there is a significant change. Once again, Bailey dramatically negates his original statements. This time, as he changes his story, we see all the witnesses who corroborated his first version ultimately contradicting his later versions. With Ian Bailey shown to be a repeat liar whose narratives are wholly unreliable, the evidence against him accumulates significantly.

80 minutes - Caught in a trap of his own making

For statements, see Appendix 2: pt 5   pt 6   pt 7

Notes

Bailey 1996- 97	Bailey 1998 and post-1998 changes
"Eddie Cassidy contacted me about murder, asked me where it was and I was able to tell him exactly as I knew Alfie Lyons....i went to the scene with Jules" Bailey 1996	"And at that time, I had no exact knowledge of the crime scene." Bailey's podcast recorded in 2022 "as an old newshound I know the local Post Office was always a good starting point and I had intended to drive there.." Bailey's own podcast recorded 2022/23
"said "How close are you to Toormore" and I said why and he said there was a murder there, a **French National**, a lady" Bailey 1997	**Non-national** (9.45am) 1998 **Non-national**, may have said French (8.02pm) 1998 Non-national, possibly French 2003 No nationality 2021
"On the road into Drinane off the Dunmanus-Toormore Rd. we met Shirley Foster coming out in her car and I spoke to her. She said are you coming to visit and I said no that the paper had called me and asked us to go to the scene." Bailey 1997	"Met Shirley at Junction of Dunmanus Road / Toormore Rd. and Drinane Road." 1998

"Stopped off at Post Office at Toormore and spoke to the Post Mistress. Checked phone book and got her name, listed there as Buinoil." Bailey 1996	"There was a few other people in the post office. Somebody came up with a name of the dead woman, I think it was Nan that mentioned a name like Bounoil they weren't sure." 1998 Nan Jermyn said they had heard the body of a French lady holiday homer had been found. Later she gave me the name Buniol the victims former married name." Big issue 2021 Nan Jermyn said that she had heard of the death and knew the victim as Sophie Buniol." Bailey podcast recorded 2022/23

CHAPTER 5

Aftermath – Post 2001
The ever-developing case against Ian Bailey

The circumstantial case against Ian Bailey is formidable. He should have been sent to trial in 2001. Had that happened, there is every prospect that he would have been found guilty of the murder of Sophie Toscan du Plantier. While there was not a criminal trial in Ireland the case did not stand still. Significant developments were relevant in terms of the case against Bailey and in terms of the content of the 2001 report. Nothing has been found that made him appear less guilty and plenty that strengthens the case against him.

The 2003-4 Civil Case

In 2003 Ian Bailey brought cases against eight British and Irish newspapers in a bid to clear his name and receive substantial damages. he had sued each newspaper for maximum circuit court damages of £26,000 that could have resulted in him receiving £208000. The trial was a disaster in more than one way for Bailey. He lost libel actions against six newspapers in January 2004 over their coverage of the brutal murder of Madame Toscan du Plantier. The two actions 'won' by Bailey were on minor points concerning his marriage in England long before the murder. The judge awarded Bailey a paltry £2800 in each case, little more than 10% of the maximum award. The £5600 awarded to him would be dwarfed by the legal costs Bailey would have to pay for losing six cases.

The damage the case inflicted on the narcissistic Bailey was more than pecuniary. At the end of the trial, the judge branded him a publicity seeker and a violent man. Few would argue with those sentiments. For seven years, the files of the Gardai investigation had remained closed and confidential, as they should have. The public knew Bailey had been arrested and questioned twice. They also knew that the DPP had concluded: " A prosecution against Bailey is not warranted by the evidence. " The assumption would be that the investigators had failed, Bailey was 'innocent', and the DPP had concluded that he had no case to answer.

The trial changed the whole dynamic concerning Bailey's potential role in the murder of Sophie. For the first time, the public became aware of many details of the case against Ian Bailey and the words of witnesses. People would also hear the conclusions reached by a senior judge who heard all the evidence. There was a paradigm shift in the way the case was perceived. Bailey could no longer pose as the poor victim of a corrupt Police force.

Justice Moran said he would have no hesitation in describing Bailey as a violent man, adding that it was "exceptional" to come across a case where a man had beaten his partner twice, let alone three times. In part three of this book, in the chapter on Similar Fact Evidence, the extent and depravity of Bailey's violence against women will be presented. The judge also commented on Bailey's personality: "One can assume that Mr. Bailey was a man who likes a certain amount of notoriety, likes to be in the limelight, and likes a bit of self-publicity." There could be little doubt that Bailey had been seen as a deeply unpleasant man.

Even more devastating than the dismantling of his character was the dismantling of his case. The judge described a series of inconsistencies in Bailey's case, adding that he accepted the evidence of witnesses who stated that Bailey had told them he killed Sophie. These witnesses included Malachi Reed and Rose and Ritchie Shelley. The judge said, "I accept that he did say that, I think it was a case of further self-publicity and was probably drink-induced." On the subject of whether Bailey met Sophie, the judge took it to be true.

The trial enabled people to see what Bailey was like, and they did not like it. They could not reconcile the evidence in the trial with the conclusion reached by the DPP in 2001. Part three of this book will provide much more evidence that the DPP got it wrong.

2011 Some important confirmations from the French investigation

In the introduction to this book, excerpts from statements given to French investigators in 2011 were introduced. The comments of the three witnesses will be presented here, along with some additional comments from Jules Thomas. Up to fifteen years after the murder, three women gave evidence that was damning for Bailey. The statements were:

Saffron Thomas

> Called JT on the 23rd wanting a lift, "probably about 11 or 12". "She (JT) said on the phone there had been a murder and she had either "been there or was going there"

Shirley Foster

> "Subsequently, he lied about it. Later, he said that he had met me at the intersection when in reality, we crossed each other halfway between the intersection and the house, at the bend."

Jules Thomas

> "We weren't sure of her name. We then went to the post office in Toormore and asked the postwoman if she knew the name of the person who lived next door to Alfie lyons. She said she thought it was BOUNIOL. It must have been around 2.30-3.00 p.m."

There were further comments by Thomas in 2011 that were particularly salient

> "We decided to head to a place where Ian had heard of a French woman. He had become aware of the presence of this Frenchwoman when he was working with Alfie LYONS"

> "We headed towards the small path that leads to the three houses. Shirley FOSTER came to us. We stopped our respective cars and talked."

Thomas confirms that Bailey knew 'exactly' where to go. It was the holiday cottage of a French woman in a remote place called Dreenane. She also refers to a small path at the end of Dreenane Lane. This meant Foster and Bailey stopped their cars on Dreenane Lane. Foster and Thomas are, in no doubt, they met on Dreenane Lane and not at the junction.

Foster and Thomas's reaffirmation in 2011 may well have precipitated Bailey's changes when giving evidence at the 2014 civil trial, referred to earlier. He once again changed his story to suggest he was not driving directly to Dreenane. This highlights how Bailey changes his story to deceive the authorities and divert attention.

The continuing lies, contradictions, and slip-ups of Ian Bailey

In the preceding chapters, we are left with no doubt that Ian Bailey has repeatedly changed his story and contradicted himself. Every time he lied, he did it to distance himself from his crimes. His lies went on after the 2001 report. There would be spikes in the number of his lies when trials or documentaries or the cold case review of Sophie's murder came along. The result of all this dishonesty and attempts to mislead people was to show that Bailey could not be trusted and he made slip-ups that pointed to his guilt.

The Irish Big Issue articles 2021

Ian Bailey originally stated he was told the body of a murdered French woman was in Toormore. In 2021, Bailey wrote a series of articles for the Big Issue Ireland. In the September issue, he said he was told there was an incident in which the body of a woman (no nationality mentioned) had been found in suspicious circumstances. There was no reference to a murder. The following month, he said he was told there had been an 'incident' – not a murder - with a non-Irish, possibly French victim. The merry-go-round of nationalities, incidents, accidents, and murder continued decades after the crime.

Take your pick - where 'exactly' becomes 'not exact knowledge' 2022

In 1996, Bailey says he knew exactly where to go to the crime scene. In his In My Own Words podcast, recorded in 2022, he stated, "And at that time, I had no exact knowledge of the crime scene." Here, twenty-six years after the murder, Bailey continued to try and change the narrative. Instead, he confirms that he is deceitful.

Ardmanagh Road 2023

Ian Bailey's last major slip-up came in his lamentable yet revealing podcast. He claimed the podcast would be his legacy. Bailey promised to leave no stone unturned in a six-episode, perfected 12-hour autobiography. The reality was three episodes that produced under two hours of material. The production was risible, and the content was often infantile.

Bailey claimed he would shock and surprise people with his content. This was certainly the case with his story about Sophie and a man who followed her on Saturday, December 21^{st,} 1996. In the second episode of the podcast, he said:

> "Significantly, Ms Farrell was to report that at the time Ms du Plantier was in her shop she observed a man wearing a dark coat and a French-style beret across the road from her shop. She further said that this man, who was about 5' 8" inches thereabouts, had subsequently followed the French visitor up the road to her parked car in Ardmanagh."
>
> Episode 2 From Paradise Lost to Paradise Found

The claim that a man followed her up Ardamanagh Road to her parked car had never been heard before the podcast. If true, it was a significant new piece of information. The issue was picked up in a blog in the summer of 2023 (https://westcorkmurderersfriends.blogspot.com) but came to greater public attention on 23.12.2023 when Barry Roche of the Irish Times, interviewed Jean-Pierre Gazeau, Sophie's uncle and President of the organisation dedicated to getting justice for her and her family.

No known statements were found that made the claims made in Bailey's podcast. Marie Farrell had made many statements to An Garda Síochána, given testimony under oath in trials, and spoken in countless on-the-record interviews. Her story had changed regularly. For all that, the content of the podcast was new. If Bailey had been aware of this in the past, he did not mention it or report it to the authorities.

The Irish Times asked Bailey about the points that Gazeau had made. He replied, "I did say that in the podcast, and I think it is provable in the statements – I'm sure it's in there in the statements somewhere, so it is provable – I wouldn't be able to put my finger exactly where it is mentioned but I know it is there and certainly it was being said around Schull at the time."

The evasiveness of Bailey's reply was not lost on anyone. He thought it was provable, that it was in the statement 'somewhere', but he was unsure where to find it. All very vague. This was part of his allegedly meticulous podcast. He had researched it and presented it. He was the self-styled 'ace' investigative journalist. Yet he had so little hard evidence that he finished off by saying it was 'being said around Schull at the time.' His best effort was that it was gossip from 27 years ago that only he remembered. If it were in the statements, why would he refer to gossip? His unease was palpable.

The story does not end there. People interested in the case on social media pushed Bailey to name the specific source. Not an unreasonable request. It was put to Bailey that AGS did not have such a statement, and if he cared about Ms du Plantier and her family, he would name the source; Bailey replied, " Ye egit.MF is on record and her statement can be found in transcripts...ye are such a psychotic ignoramus." Amidst his insults, Bailey had failed to name a specific source. When pressed again a third time, he replied, "He should read MF's Statements and testimony in Historic Case." Another meaningless reply.

There was little doubt that Bailey had lied about what Farrell had said and lied about there being some statements to that effect. This was typical of the man. He lied in 1996, and he was still lying in 2024. It was an almost childlike attempt to misdirect everyone. It resulted in him appearing more guilty. If he knew Sophie's car was on Ardamanagh Road and she was followed to it by a man, then that man was most likely Ian Bailey. One would hope that even the most committed 'Bailey is innocent' person at the DPP would recognise that Bailey had always lied about the case, his lies could never be corroborated and he duped people in their organisation.

Since the instigation of the cold case review of the murder of Sophie Toscan du Plantier, there has been new evidence and new leads. All indications are that what has been uncovered lends greater support to the conclusion that Ian Bailey murdered Sophie.

CHAPTER **6**

December 21st to 23rd 1996 - reasonable inferences

In chapter one the basis of a circumstantial case was explained. In the absence of direct evidence, the case of Sophie's murder will be, by necessity, circumstantial. This is true for many serious crimes. The content of the book so far describes the significant, indeed compelling, case that can be made against Ian Bailey. When reading about the changes Bailey made in his story, remember that in 2001, the DPP denied extensive changes; they said there were some errors.

Ian Bailey's original narrative	Ian Bailey's original narrative – items he changed in bold with a line through
Ian Bailey told the police that on the Saturday before Sophie Toscan du Plantier was murdered, he spent the evening at home at the Prairie Cottage. He got up on Sunday morning and killed some turkeys in preparation for selling them.	~~Ian Bailey told the police that on the Saturday before Sophie Toscan du Plantier was murdered, he spent the evening at home at the Prairie Cottage.~~ ~~He got up on Sunday morning and killed some turkeys in preparation for selling them.~~

He first claimed that he and Saffron Thomas went and cut the top off a tree on the morning of the 22nd.	He first claimed that he and Saffron Thomas went and cut the top off a tree on the morning of the 22nd.
	[He also changed the times the tree was cut down and who participated. See chapter 7]
He said he had received scratches and injuries while doing these tasks.	He said he had received scratches and injuries while doing these tasks.
	[gave 2 versions of events. In one it was cuts via the saw.in the other it was scratches. Multiple versions of how he got his head cut]
He went on to say that on the evening of Sunday, December 22nd, he went into Schull with his partner Jules Thomas to visit the bars.	He went on to say that on the evening of Sunday, December 22nd, he went into Schull with his partner Jules Thomas to visit the bars.
He said that around midnight he and Thomas left the Courtyard bar and, though intoxicated, drove straight home by the the most direct route possible.	He said that around midnight he and Thomas left the Courtyard bar and, though intoxicated, drove straight home by the t most direct route possible.
On arrival at home, he said he and Thomas went to bed around 01.00 to 01.30	On arrival at home, he said he and Thomas went to bed around 01.00 to 01.30
	[gave a completely new story about the venue/route taken/ stopping and getting out of the car]

December 21st to 23rd 1996 - reasonable inferences

and remained in bed until 08.00 to 09.00 on the morning of December 23rd.	~~and remained in bed until 08.00 to 09.00 on the morning of December 23rd.~~
At that time Bailey says he got up and made coffee for himself and Jues Thomas and returned to bed. He says they put on the radio and listened to it until approximately 10.00. while in bed he says they planned their visit to Skibbereen that afternoon. Bailey then says he got up and spent the rest of his time 'pottering around' until he got a phone call from journalist Eddie Cassidy.	~~At that time Bailey says he got up and made coffee for himself and Jules Thomas and returned to bed. He says they put on the radio and listened to it until approximately 10.00. while in bed he says they planned their visit to Skibbereen that afternoon.~~ ~~Bailey then says he got up and spent the rest of his time 'pottering around' until he got a phone call from journalist Eddie Cassidy.~~ [His story changed the facts twenty times and included a false alibi]
Bailey says that Cassidy told him a French woman had been murdered	~~Bailey says that Cassidy told him a French woman had been murdered~~ [Changed it to non-national possibly French and other variations]
locally and asked him to do some work on this story.	locally and asked him to do some work on this story.

Bailey said that when Cassidy gave him the details he knew exactly where to find the deceased.	~~Bailey said that when Cassidy gave him the details he knew exactly where to find the deceased.~~ [This story was changed more than once]
He says he knew this because he had done some labouring work for an English man, Alf Lyons, eighteen months earlier and he had a French neighbour who had a holiday cottage nearby.	~~He says he knew this because he had done some labouring work for an English man, Alf Lyons, eighteen months earlier and he had a French neighbour who had a holiday cottage nearby.~~
Bailey told Thomas about his call and after a few phone calls made to newspaper contacts,	Bailey told Thomas about his call and after a few phone calls made to newspaper contacts,
he drove directly to the cottages in Dreenane.	~~he drove directly to the cottages in Dreenane.~~
Approximately half-way along a secluded single-track lane that led only to the Dreenane cottages Bailey met Shirley Foster, the partner of Alfie Lyons, travelling in the opposite direction.	~~Approximately halfway along a secluded single-track lane that led only to the Dreenane cottages Bailey met Shirley Foster, the partner of Alfie Lyons, travelling in the opposite direction.~~

December 21st to 23rd 1996 - reasonable inferences

At the scene of the crime, Bailey was able to see in the distance where the covered body of a deceased person was found. He was referred by the officers on the scene to contact the AGS press office for further information. Bailey and Thomas then left and drove to the Post Office at Toormore.	At the scene of the crime, Bailey was able to see in the distance where the covered body of a deceased person was found. He was referred by the officers on the scene to contact the AGS press office for further information. Bailey and Thomas then left and drove to the Post Office at Toormore.
There Bailey asked if they had the name of the French woman who owned the cottage at Dreenane. They got her name from the phone book. Bailey then returned home.	~~There Bailey asked if they had the name of the French woman who owned the cottage at Dreenane. They got her name from the phone book. Bailey then returned home.~~
Ian Bailey's original narrative	Ian Bailey's original narrative – items he changed in bold with a line through
Ian Bailey told the police that on the Saturday before Sophie Toscan du Plantier was murdered, he spent the evening at home at the Prairie Cottage. He got up on Sunday morning and killed some turkeys in preparation for selling them.	~~Ian Bailey told the police that on the Saturday before Sophie Toscan du Plantier was murdered, he spent the evening at home at the Prairie Cottage. He got up on Sunday morning and killed some turkeys in preparation for selling them.~~

He first claimed that he and Saffron Thomas went and cut the top off a tree on the morning of the 22nd.	~~He also claims that he and Saffron Thomas went and cut the top off a tree on the morning of the~~ *[Also said it was the afternoon of the 22nd or the 23rd possibly with Virginia]*
He said he had received scratches and injuries while doing these tasks.	~~He said he had received scratches and injuries while doing these tasks.~~ *[gave 2 versions of events. I none it was cuts via the saw.in the other it was scratches. Multiple versions of how he got his head cut]*
He went on to say that on the evening of Sunday, December 22^{nd,} he went into Schull with his partner Jules Thomas to visit the bars.	He went on to say that on the evening of Sunday, December 22^{nd,} he went into Schull with his partner Jules Thomas to visit the bars.
He said that around midnight he and Thomas left the Courtyard bar and, though intoxicated, drove straight home by the the most direct route possible.	~~He said that around midnight he and Thomas left the Courtyard bar and, though intoxicated, drove straight home by the t most direct route possible.~~
On arrival at home, he said he and Thomas went to bed around 01.00 to 01.30	On arrival at home, he said he and Thomas went to bed around 01.00 to 01.30 *[gave a completely new story about the venue/route taken/ stopping and getting out of the car]*

December 21st to 23rd 1996 - reasonable inferences

and remained in bed until 08.00 to 09.00 on the morning of December 23rd.	~~and remained in bed until 08.00 to 09.00 on the morning of December 23rd.~~
At that time Bailey says he got up and made coffee for himself and Jues Thomas and returned to bed. He says they put on the radio and listened to it until approximately 10.00. while in bed he says they planned their visit to Skibbereen that afternoon. Bailey then says he got up and spent the rest of his time 'pottering around' until he got a phone call from journalist Eddie Cassidy.	~~At that time Bailey says he got up and made coffee for himself and Jules Thomas and returned to bed. He says they put on the radio and listened to it until approximately 10.00. while in bed he says they planned their visit to Skibbereen that afternoon.~~ ~~Bailey then says he got up and spent the rest of his time 'pottering around' until he got a phone call from journalist Eddie Cassidy.~~ [His story changed the facts twenty times and included a false alibi]
Bailey says that Cassidy told him a French woman had been murdered	~~Bailey says that Cassidy told him a French woman had been murdered~~ [Changed it to non-national possibly French and other variations]

locally and asked him to do some work on this story.	locally and asked him to do some work on this story.
Bailey said that when Cassidy gave him the details he knew exactly where to find the deceased.	~~Bailey said that when Cassidy gave him the details he knew exactly where to find the deceased.~~
	[This story was changed more than once]
He says he knew this because he had done some labouring work for an English man, Alfie Lyons, eighteen months earlier and he had a French neighbour who had a holiday cottage nearby.	~~He says he knew this because he had done some labouring work for an English man, Alfie Lyons, eighteen months earlier and he had a French neighbour who had a holiday cottage nearby.~~
Bailey told Thomas about his call and After a few phone calls made to newspaper contacts,	Bailey told Thomas about his call and after a few phone calls made to newspaper contacts,
he drove directly to the cottages in Dreenane.	~~he drove directly to the cottages in Dreenane.~~
Approximately half-way along a secluded single-track lane that led only to the Dreenane cottages Bailey met Shirley Foster, the partner of Alf Lyons, travelling in the opposite direction.	~~Approximately halfway along a secluded single-track lane that led only to the Dreenane cottages Bailey met Shirley Foster, the partner of Alf Lyons, travelling in the opposite direction.~~

December 21st to 23rd 1996 - reasonable inferences   **93**

| At the scene of the crime, Bailey was able to see in the distance where the covered body of a deceased person was found. He was referred by the officers on the scene to contact the AGS press office for further information. Bailey and Thomas then left and drove to the Post Office at Toormore. | At the scene of the crime, Bailey was able to see in the distance where the covered body of a deceased person was found. He was referred by the officers on the scene to contact the AGS press office for further information. Bailey and Thomas then left and drove to the Post Office at Toormore. |
| There Bailey asked if they had the name of the French woman who owned the cottage at Dreenane. They got her name from the phone book. Bailey then returned home. | ~~There Bailey asked if they had the name of the French woman who owned the cottage at Dreenane. They got her name from the phone book. Bailey then returned home.~~ |

With so many lies being told by Bailey about what he did, where he was, and what he said, there is ample evidence demonstrating his culpability. This is not all there is. In chapter three, the true events of the morning of the 23rd are spelled out, showing Bailey and Thomas knew about the murder long before the call from Eddie Cassidy and before Shirley Foster found Sophie. There are also the many changes Bailey continued to make in an attempt to distance himself from what he knew and what he did.

What we know and what can be inferred from these facts

What we know

1. Ian Bailey lied repeatedly about where he was and what he did on the evening and night of December 21st, 1996.
2. Ian Bailey lied about where he was and what he did from morning until noon on December 22nd, 1996.
3. There have been contradictions and falsehoods about the timings and days of the turkey killings and tree chopping on December 22nd and or 23rd.
4. Lies were told about the bar Bailey and Thomas left the route home, and whether they stopped on the way home in the first hour of 23.12.1996.
5. Bailey and Thomas lied about his actions between 1 am and 8 am on 23.12.1996. This was the false alibi claiming he was in bed with Jules Thomas at the time Sophie was murdered.
6. Once his false alibi collapsed, his story changed at least 20 times about what he was doing the morning of 23.12.1996, and he said nothing to investigators about what he did between 11 am and 1.40 pm. Most, if not all, of what he said about that morning was untrue.
7. Bailey changed his story about what Eddie Cassidy told him at 1.40 pm on 23.12.1996 regarding the nationality of the deceased woman. He said he was told there was an incident, accident, and, at other times, a murder. This means the majority of what he said was untrue, possibly all of it.

8. Bailey told Eddie Cassidy he knew the exact location of the dead woman and told AGS a detailed story to explain why he knew where the victim must be. He drove straight to the scene of the crime.
9. Bailey changed his story on knowing where to find the victim, where he was driving to on the morning of the 23rd, changed the location of where he met Shirley Foster, and changed his whole story on why he later went to the Post Office.
10. Bailey's narrative for what he did between 1 am and 1.40 pm on 23.12.1996 is a mass of contradictions, evasions, and lies. It is uncorroborated. An alternative timeline based on the evidence of at least 12 witnesses shows that Bailey was already aware of the location of the scene of the crime and who the victim was early that morning. The witnesses comprise of two members of the Thomas family, four experienced newspapermen, a market trader, a teacher, a local business owner, two other local people getting on with their lives that morning and Jules Thomas. Many of these people knew others by sight or not at all yet their individual statements corroborate each other's.
11. After the call from Cassidy, and according to Bailey, he and Thomas drove directly to the scene of the crime without making any further inquiries. After a fleeting visit there, Bailey drove to the post office to ask for the name of the French cottage owner, the deceased woman. Bailey's version was corroborated by other witnesses. From 1998 onwards, Bailey completely

changed his story. He made changes up until his death in 2024. The original version implicated him. No one else changed their story. Most notably Jules Thomas, Shirley Foster, Ann Dukelow, and Nan Jermyn.

What can be inferred from these facts?

An inference is not itself evidence. It is the result of logical reasoning from the evidence. The law treats it with as much strength and validity as direct evidence. Reasonable inference means "conclusions which are regarded as logical by reasonable people in the light of their experience in life."

A. What logical and reasonable inferences may be made about a man who
   - gave the Police a false alibi?
   - repeatedly made false statements?
   - continuously changed his story, particularly when he is caught in a lie?
   - knew exactly where to find a body in a remote location when given vague and basic details?
   - knew the identity of a murdered woman when he had not been told who she was?
   - spent years creating false stories because his original versions implicated him?

B. What logical and reasonable inferences may be made about a man and a woman who
- knew about the murder before the body was found and before the Police officers reached the scene of the crime?
- told 4 people about the murder and 2 people about visiting the scene of the crime hours before they were officially informed about the incident.

Ian Bailey was a journalist. It could have been he had been given information about a French woman who was murdered close to her holiday home in Dreenane in the early hours of 23.12.1996 by a confidential source. If so, he could have immediately informed An Garda Síochána so that they could start their investigations as soon as possible. As a self-styled, highly regarded, and experienced investigative journalist, he would know that the quicker a crime is discovered, the better it is for investigators. So why did he hang on for hours? It would also be possible that his informant could be the perpetrator or know other vital pieces of information. However, he failed to inform the police.

C. What logical and reasonable inferences may be made about a journalist who, if he knew the things listed in A and B early in the day, yet failed to

- immediately inform An Garda Síochána plus
- immediately commence further investigations, including contacting news agencies

Bailey had a case to answer. Based on the evidence so far, he should have been charged and sent to trial. He would have almost certainly been found guilty.

There is more evidence to come, and none of it helps Bailey.

PART TWO
The growing evidence against Ian Bailey

CHAPTER 7

The case of the disappearing and reappearing scratches

The scene of the crime where Sophie Toscan du Plantier was savagely murdered was one of brutal carnage. The presence of briars and brambles accentuated the horror. These briars had thorns that were capable of inflicting scratches and deep cuts. For this reason, it was reasonable to infer that the murderer would be likely to suffer injuries if his bare skin came into contact with these cutting plants. In most cases, the bare skin would be the face, hands, and possibly forearms.

There is a consensus that Bailey did indeed have a noteworthy number of scratches on his hands and arms and a cut to the head from December 23[rd,] 1996, onwards. Several people independently reported the scratches observed from December 23rd onwards. The witnesses included Thomas family house guest Arianna Boarina. She said the damage to Bailey's hands and arms was inconsistent with cutting the top of a small tree (as he would later claim). They looked more like the injuries caused by briars that she had seen in her hometown in Italy. Denis O'Callaghan saw Bailey on 24 December 1996 - the day after the murder. He noticed multiple light scratches on Bailey's arms. Also, on the 24th, a shop assistant saw scratches, mainly on Bailey's left hand.

On December 27th, in Brosnan's Spar supermarket in Schull, Gard Bart O'Leary noticed the back of both of Bailey's hands covered in what appeared to him to be briar marks. Gard Kevin Kelleher was also present. He noted seeing light scratches extending over Bailey's left wrist. The following day, O'Leary and Kelleher – visited the Prairie cottage. On closer investigation, O'Leary observed scratches on both forearms and both hands; the scratches were forming scabs, indicating that the original cuts had happened several days earlier; they also noted a cut to the head that was not a scratch. At the time, Bailey said the head cut was caused by the flying 'talon' of a turkey when it was being slaughtered.

The scratch to the head on Bailey was unseen on the 22nd but observed by Jules Thomas sometime after 9 am on the 23rd of December. She did not see it when she went to bed with Bailey at 1.30 am. Bailey said he had hurt himself with a stick. One moment, it is a killer turkey; the next, an inanimate stick. more gibberish from Bailey.

Jules Thomas and her daughters Saffron and Virginia all attested to Ian Bailey's scratch-like injuries on his arms and hands. This means Bailey's family members, Police officers, shop assistants, and a guest are all in agreement. Bailey had noticeable injuries.

This is why the issue of scratches and cuts on Ian Bailey's hands and arms became such an important consideration in this murder case. The primary question became: when and where did Ian Bailey sustain his scratches and injuries?

If Ian Bailey left the Galley bar in Schull close to midnight on December 22nd, 1996, without the discernible scratches seen by witnesses on the 23rd, then he would be compelled to explain where he got them. A jury would be free to draw inferences about the cause of the scratches. Alternatively, if Bailey had the scratches seen on the 23rd while in the bar, the injuries came earlier that day and could not be related to the crime scene.

Ian Bailey attributed his damaged hands and arms to injuries incurred while killing turkeys and felling the top of a Christmas tree on December 22nd. The statements allegedly supporting this narrative came from five people: Bailey, his partner Jules Thomas, and her three daughters – Saffron, Virginia, and Fenella. This was the story coming solely from the occupants of the Prairie cottage. No one outside the 'Thomas-Bailey family' confirms his story.

The alternative narrative is that Bailey left the Galley with near zero or zero injuries and that he must have been scratched and cut after midnight. Many witnesses observed this scenario in the Galley on the 22nd. This group of people included the owners, staff, and customers, who came from a wide range of backgrounds.

A deep dive into the statements highlights a distinct difference between the 'Prairie evidence' and the 'Galley evidence'. The Prairie evidence is highly contradictory, conflicting, and inconsistent, while the Galley evidence is confirmatory, corroborative, and consistent. For too long, the Prairie evidence has been treated as if it was coherent and provided a strong defence of Ian Bailey. This is patently untrue.

Not only does it provide no meaningful defence for Bailey, but it also raises questions about the statements that were made.

The Prairie evidence - the assertion Bailey had a significant number of scratches and cuts on the 22nd

All the witnesses allegedly corroborating Bailey's claim that he had scratches on the 22nd. lived in the same home. One was his long-term partner, Jules Thomas. The other three were the daughters of Jules:Saffron, Virginia and Fenella. Not a single person outside the Prairie corroborated Bailey's narrative. Given the events of the killing of turkeys and chopping the top of a tree are not complex events, and they were recent, one would expect the Prairie occupants to be able to give consistent, corroborating accounts of what happened. A superficial reading of the Prairie statements may suggest corroborating accounts, but closer scrutiny reveals a disjointed and chaotic hotchpotch of narratives.

Timings - When were the turkeys killed and the tree chopped down?

One would expect the timings of the killing and chopping events to be easy to establish and agree upon. These were notable daytime events in the sober, cold light of day. In most cases, they were being recalled just a few days or weeks after they occurred. However, in this case the reality is far from the expectation.

The case of the disappearing and reappearing scratches 105

In his signed statement of 31.12.1996, Ian Bailey says that the tree was chopped down on the morning of December 22nd with the assistance of Saffron. Then, at lunchtime, he said he killed three turkeys. This statement was given in the days after the events allegedly took place. They were given by a journalist whose trade is to provide precise details of events. When arrested and interviewed on 10.02.1997, Bailey dramatically changed his story.

He had little option but to change. This is because he had told the Police a series of lies about what he had been doing on the night of December 21st and the entire morning of the 22nd. He was in Schull at the time he claimed to have cut down the tree and killed the turkeys on Sunday morning. It would have been impossible for Bailey and Saffron Thomas to be cutting down a tree that morning.

Bailey had knowingly lied about the timing of those events. He would subsequently make significant changes in his story. In all future narratives, he would kill the turkeys first and then cut down the tree. In a trial, he would have needed to explain why he had lied to the police about this, as he had with many other issues. In his second version of events, Bailey admitted he did not get home until 12.30 pm. It was probably a little later. This time, the turkeys were allegedly killed first, and then the tree was cut down.

Other important variations in the story are irreconcilable. In the February 1997 statement, Bailey says, " But Jules and Saffy arrived back just after I killed the Turkey's." Interviewed on the same day, Saffron Thomas stated, "We had to kill three turkeys, and in doing so, Ian was caught by the turkey's wings flapping when their heads were cut off." In 2002, Saffron Thomas stated, "He hadn't these scratches before he started and must have got them from the turkeys and the cutting of the tree. It would not be unusual to have scratches from killing the turkeys because they flap around so much while killing them when they were dying."

In the first quote, Bailey says Saffron was not there, but in the second quote, Saffron gives a very descriptive account of him killing the turkeys. In the third quote, Ms Thomas offers a more general description, as if she were not there. If present, she could have described the specific injuries. If this was not confusing and contradictory enough, the statement made by Jules Thomas on 10.02.1997 made it more so. She said she was there before the killing and makes no reference to Saffron being present and helping.

Three people, three contradictory stories. Once scrutinised, these tales do not offer a coherent narrative. A thin veneer of corroboration gives way to significant inconsistencies and contradictions. These are three separate stories. To believe one necessitates disbelieving the other two. This raises the distinct possibility that none of these narratives should be believed. This issue alone makes the Prairie narrative very hard to believe. It gets worse for Bailey.

Timings – Even Bigger changes

In the 2003 civil trial, Ian Bailey and Jules Thomas were answering questions under oath. Amazingly, the time of the activities did not move a few hours from morning to afternoon; they were now said to have happened on a completely different day. At one point, Bailey was being questioned by his counsel. This would mean he had a good idea of what would be put to him when asked what he was doing before a phone call on the 23rd. Bailey answered - "The turkeys were being prepared for the table. I had to kill them. But I got one small scratch from a talon as I did the job. I used a knife."

This is no slip of the tongue. He knew the question was coming. Had the barrister thought there was an error, he would have re-stated the question to enable Bailey to 'correct' his initial reply. In the same trial, Jules Thomas also confirmed that the turkey killing was on the 23rd. A document was produced to the court of a complaint by Ms Thomas to the chief State solicitor's office about the accuracy of her signed statement. In it, she said that details such as the raw bloody scratch were "fiction," and it was later on the day of the murder, the 23rd, that Bailey had got some scratches after killing a turkey and chopping down a Christmas tree.

The court case was not the only time Bailey claimed the tree chopping was on the 23rd. In a note sent by Bailey to his family in England, he stated that the tree was cut down on the 23rd. He also told Caroline Mangèz, the Paris Match journalist, that he killed the turkeys on the 23rd of December.

The statements made by the Prairie witnesses are confusing and appear unreliable on something as basic as when a task was undertaken.

Who helped chop down the tree? - Saffy and Virginia

Bailey and the Thomas women cannot be relied upon as to when the turkey killing and tree chopping occurred. There is also plenty of confusion regarding who undertook these activities. The main narrative has Bailey and Saffron Thomas cutting down the tree. When the tree is transported from where it is cut down back to the Prairie, the story says Saffron drove the short distance home while Bailey transported it back. However, Liam O'Driscoll, a man who met Bailey on his way home with the tree, was clear on three points. First, Bailey was not alone; he was accompanied by a young woman. Second, it was not Saffron Thomas. O'Driscoll had given Saffron a lift many times and knew her. Third, the woman had dark hair, and he believed her to be Saffron's sister. Suddenly, Virginia appears to be involved,

In Virginia's statement about the cutting down of the tree, she states, ". Ian also climbed to the top of a tree to cut the top off to use as a Christmas tree. I did see his hands scratched when he came down the tree." She places herself at the cutting down of the tree. Yet in all the accounts of the tree chopping alleged on the 22[nd,] none of the others ever mentioned Virginia. In all the statements by Bailey, Jules Thomas, and Saffron Thomas, there is no mention of Virginia helping Bailey and Saffron. If she was not there, then her statement cannot be true. If she was there, as Liam O'Driscoll strongly suggests, why did no one else mention it?

Other statements further complicate this chaotic scenario. Saffron's boyfriend at the time described a visit to her father, Michael Oliver, that Christmas. He says she told her Dad the scratches on her hands were from cutting down a Christmas tree. Saffron added that Bailey had not cut down the tree and was lying if he said otherwise. Michael Oliver told gardaí that his daughter told him that Ian Bailey was "a lazy bastard" and that he did not even want to get them a Christmas tree. She explained she had to cut the tree and took it to the house herself. If these statements were believed, then it meant that Bailey did not take part in cutting down the tree. This would mean any scratches happened elsewhere.

What would any sane person infer from the stories told by the occupants of the Prairie? They could infer that there is no common ground between the witnesses. There is only confusion.

The scratches

At the heart of this evidential mishmash is, of course, the issue of the scratches or cuts that Bailey was said to have received while killing turkeys and chopping down a tree. One would expect that this element would present a clear description of Bailey's injuries and that these injuries would closely match the injuries reported by witnesses who saw Bailey from the 23rd onwards. It would be a straightforward process of the four Thomas women and Bailey observing the harm done and reporting it accurately.

If there was a match then it may be possible to infer that the turkey and tree injuries could account for the injuries people reported from December 23rd and later. If the scratches described from the 23rd were in excess of those reported by Bailey and the Thomas's then it is possible to infer that some other events caused the additional injuries.

First, it is necessary to see if this gang of five witnessed the same injuries. They did not. Ian Bailey makes reference to the injuries in his 1996 statement, while Jules Thomas does not mention them in 1996. What he says and does not say is revealing. All he says is he cut himself with a bow saw, and the cuts healed. That is it. There is no reference to any injuries incurred while killing the turkeys nor any reference to an injury above his eye. He is specific. He cut himself with a bow saw. There is no reference to getting scratched by any possible means. This is very strange because everyone agrees that, whatever the source, Bailey had scratches on his hands and arms. Yet he does not tell the investigators about any scratches. At that time, he was one of many people who gave a statement. He was not a suspect, so why would an honest man withhold information? If he, as he claimed, got scratches while doing Christmas chores, then why mislead the Police? In the earlier chapters we saw how Bailey's statement of 31.12.1996 was a tissue of lies. He appears to be a stranger to the truth.

In the next series of statements around February 1997, all the people claiming Bailey had scratches on the 22nd proffer comments on what happened to him. He said he was slightly marked and got more scratches later. He said nothing about the location or severity of the scratches. He was being rather vague. He does not refer to getting a deep cut on his forehead over his eye. His partner, Jules Thomas, said there were scratches on his forearms. She does not refer to the cut over his eye nor scratches on any other part of Bailey's body. In particular, she does not reference cuts on the hands. This was not the same story told by Bailey. Saffron had a third and yet another different story. For her, it was not a vague reference to some scratches or scratches limited to the forearms. It was hands, arms, and legs. Bailey was scratched everywhere. Later, in 2002, Saffron says he was scratched on his arms. The legs and hands were no longer mentioned. This contrasts with Virginia, who said only the hands were scratched when Bailey descended from the tree. However, we don't know if Virginia was ever there. A fifth witness was the youngest of the three daughters, Fenella Thomas. She saw no scratches. Fenella saw some marks on Bailey's nose. Five witnesses and five different tales of the injuries.

So far, Bailey changed his statement on injuries between 1996 and 1997, making them appear worse. Saffron changed her statements between 1997 and 2002, making them less severe. In both cases, each person has contradicted their own evidence.

10.02.1997 statements on injuries plus later statements

IKB	JT	ST	VT	FT
Slightly marked More scratches later No location of scratches	Forearms scratched	cuts and scratches to his hands, arms and legs	his hands scratched	
No mention of the head	Nothing of the head [JT did not see a scratch to the head until the 23rd Bailey attributed it to his big stick]	No mention of the head	No mention of the head	
1996 Cut with bow saw, cuts healed		2002 had scratches on his arms and he *might* even have had a scratch around his eyebrow.		2002 There were definitely marks on his nose. That's the best I can remember.

Many of the statements were made within weeks of the murder. While four witnesses refer to scratches, there are significant variations. They are not describing the same thing. This unreliable and unbelievable narrative about scratches was maintained for decades. However, it should be acknowledged that Ian Bailey stated on October 12th, 2023, "There weren't any scratches on my hands." In this case, Bailey contradicts Jules, her daughter's bar Fenella, and everyone who reported seeing scratches from December 23rd, 1996. How could any balanced person or juror trust a word out of his mouth?

Inconsistent and conflicting statements

In eight signed statements plus evidence by Bailey and Jules Thomas in 2003, there are significant contradictions on the timings of the turkey killings and tree cutting, contradictions on who was involved, and conflicting evidence on Bailey's alleged injuries. The Prairie people contradict themselves and each other. It resembles a situation where people agree on the broad principles of a narrative while filling in their details individually. It is a free-for-all. Plus, evidence from others suggests that Bailey played no part in chopping down the tree. Even the most unremarkable barrister would revel in the opportunities to expose so many inconsistencies, contradictions, and outright lies. The Prairie evidence fails to provide a single believable coherent narrative.

The Galley evidence - The assertion Bailey had no scratches on the 22nd

There is no suggestion that Ian Bailey's murder of Sophie Toscan du Plantier was premeditated. It was most likely a spontaneous act triggered by events at or near Sophie's cottage in the very early hours of 23.12.1996. He did not know he was going to murder her. He did not know how he would do it, and nor did he know that the place of her murder would have sharp thorns. So, on the night of the murder, the behaviour of the frequently drunk Ian Bailey was much like many, possibly all, of his nights out in Schull.

On the previous evening, he had drunk heavily and more than likely taken drugs. Though feckless and incapable of holding down a full-time job, he was able to feed his addictions because of the pocket money he received from Thomas. On Sunday evening, he was, once again, drunk.

He liked to perform in front of people when sober, more so when drunk. On many occasions, people going out for a convivial evening with friends would be endlessly interrupted when Bailey insisted on loudly proclaiming his appalling poetry to an unfortunate audience. He thought he was entertaining the people there. This simultaneously proved he had no idea how dreadful his poetry was, and his inability to read the responses of an audience. On the night of the 22nd, Bailey decided to 'treat' his audience in the Galley bar by playing a bodhran. A bodhran is an Irish frame drum. He fancied himself a gifted drum player, but he was not. With sleeves rolled up that night, he banged away and danced around. He could not be missed. Soon, we will look at what people observed in the bar and what they did not see.

What Liam O'Driscoll did not see

Liam O'Driscoll told the police that he saw Ian Bailey and a young woman (not Saffron and possibly Virginia) taking a Christmas tree toward the Prairie cottage. He did not witness Bailey cutting down the tree or him carrying a large bow saw. His comments appeared observant enough. What is of interest here is another thing he did not see. Namely, many recent raw bloody wounds on Bailey's hands and arms – and potentially on his legs. There was no mention of scratches and cuts. This point should be considered when evaluating people's statements in the Galley bar on the late evening of December 22nd.

The bodhran player in the bar

A significant part of Bailey's evening on December 22^{nd,} 1996, was spent at the Galley bar. While there, he did not sit quietly in the corner sipping a few drinks and chatting with Jules Thomas. He was his usual loud self, keen to perform for those people present. The barman, John McGowan, gave a statement to the Police on 22.02.1997. He told them, " I remember serving drinks to Ian Bailey four or five times during the course of the night. The bar counter is well lit, and I saw his hands and face well. I am sure there were no scratches to his face or hands; if there were any, I would have noticed. When he was paying for the drink, he counted out his change. He spent some time at it as he was short, at about 20p. I saw his hands well while he was doing this."

McGowan explained to the Police that he had seen an article in the Examiner the week before his statement. The article offered the story that Ian Bailey had scratches on his face and hands as a result of killing turkeys and cutting a Christmas tree on Sunday, the 22nd. McGowan said it struck him that he had seen no such thing that Sunday night. In a statement on February 20th, the publican David Galvin said there were no marks on Bailey's face on the night of the 22nd.

In further statements made on February 4th, 1997, two people seated close to Bailey saw no indications of injury on him. Sinead Kelly said, "On Sunday 22nd December 1996, I didn't notice any marks or scratches on the hands or face of the gent that had the Bodhran when he was seated near us." Bernadette Kelly went into greater detail. She observed drink marks around his mouth and that he appeared scruffier than usual with a rough, stubbly face. She saw no scratches. These are people saying what they saw that evening. Both were seated close to Bailey and saw no evidence of injuries.

The Kellys were not alone in their observations of Ian Bailey. Another customer, Christy Lynch, told the police that he saw no injuries on Bailey's hands or face. Customer Paul O'Regan stated, " I didn't notice anything unusual about him, and I didn't notice any scratches or marks on him."

Finally, Venita Roche Galvin was also interviewed in February 1997. She was the publican's wife. She could not have been clearer. She saw Bailey up close and in a well-lit

The case of the disappearing and reappearing scratches 117

area. They spoke briefly. She added, "I did not notice any marks on his face, and I think if there were any marks on his face, I would have noticed them. I can't recall seeing any marks on his hands." Venita Galvin had also read a later story about Bailey's injuries and recalled that he had no injuries on the night of the 22nd in the bar.

One customer, Richard Tisdall, did see some signs of an injury. He first stated that the man playing the Bodhran was sitting approximately six feet away from him. He said he noticed no scratches on Bailey's hands, forearms, or face. Later, Tisdall changed his story, saying Bailey had scratches on one of his hands but nowhere else. His description of a slight injury to one hand is nothing like all the descriptions of Bailey's injuries by people who saw him from December 23rd onwards. Even if Tisdall was accurate, Bailey incurred further significant injuries after he left the Galley Bar that night.

This situation is even curiouser. If Jules Thomas and Tisdall are to be believed, then Bailey scratched his forearms and both hands on the afternoon of the 22nd. By the evening of the 22nd, all the forearm scratches and scratches on one hand became invisible, leaving Tisdall to see only scratches of some kind on one hand. Then, after leaving the bar at midnight, all the original scratches and maybe some others became visible from the 23rd onwards. If the unanimous statements of the Galvins, the Kellys, McGowan, Lynch, and O'Regan are believed, there were no cuts or scratches that evening. This would mean the five Prairie witnesses expect people to believe Bailey was injured in the afternoon, the injuries became invisible in the evening and they reappeared the next day. Would any jury believe such nonsense?

This would not be just an astonishing series of events for this case it would be an astonishing case study for the medical sciences. Either that or Bailey had zero or near-zero scratches when he entered and later left the Galley bar that night.

The seven witnesses in the bar who saw no injuries were not some scheming group working with the police. They had not colluded. They did not have a reason to lie about what they had seen. They made their statements and their observations in good faith. They do not contradict each other, and there are no indications that they lied. Richard Tisdall says he saw a scratch or scratches on one hand alone. Even if this were to be accepted, the injuries seen and described regarding the 23rd and afterward were significantly more severe than what Tisdall described. The question remains: how did Bailey get all the additional scratches?

Scratches after midnight

The Prairie evidence is replete with repeated inconsistencies, self-contradictions, contradictions of each other, and changes made by Bailey and the other occupants. It is impossible to ignore the many disagreements about when the turkey and tree work was done, who did it, and what injuries they allege Bailey suffered. This is in sharp contrast with the consistent statements from everyone in the Galley bar. They say Bailey was essentially injury-free when he left the bar. A jury would have been asked to select the narrative that they believed to be true. While a jury never got the chance to make that decision. You can make up your mind.

The Galley evidence is clear. Ian Bailey did not have significant scratches to his face, arms, and hands in the bar on 22.12.1996. He never accounted for how he got them. He did not get them while 'sleeping' through the entire night, while writing in the kitchen, walking to and from the Studio, listening to the radio in bed with Thomas, or any of the other convoluted uncorroborated false narratives he cared to concoct.

He had injuries consistent with an attack on Ms du Plantier and no plausible and consistent explanation of how he received his injuries in the light of the Galley bar evidence. It is both reasonable and logical to infer that his injuries came after midnight and sometime during the early hours of December 23rd.

For statements, see Appendix 2: pt 8

CHAPTER 8

The case of the invisible confessions

There can be few people who have confessed to a specific murder more times than Ian Bailey. No one else appears to have confessed to this murder, and Bailey has never confessed to other murders. Indeed, he confesses to no other criminal activities. Yet regarding the murder of Sophie Toscan du Plantier, he did so, many times. In Ireland, the DPP sided with Ian Bailey and dismissed every single confession. In France, however, the court accepted the confessions as real. Likewise, in an Irish civil trial in 2003, the Judge believed the evidence that Bailey confessed. This would mean Ian Bailey admitted to the murder of Sophie. Who to believe? The DPP decided that a jury should not consider who was most believable, Bailey or the people reporting the confessions.

Since the murder of Sophie Toscan du Plantier, one man has confessed to the murder on several occasions. Confessing to a variety of people of different ages in various settings. Unsurprisingly, that man is Ian Bailey.

These are all voluntary confessions. They are not the result of force, coercion, or intimidation. Bailey spoke freely. Confessions like this tend to be made for two main reasons. Some people are driven by guilt and remorse. The perpetrator finds it increasingly difficult to live with their criminal actions. The opportunity to tell somebody, anybody, what they have done can help reduce stress and anxiety.

The second reason stems more from narcissism and a desire for notoriety. These people are bursting to tell someone. It is not enough that they have done something vile; they need to revel in their depravity. Whether they make admissions or create pantomimes for later denial, they aim to be front and centre, connected with the crime.

Paris 2019

In the 2019 trial, the French court initially focused on four instances of Ian Bailey confessing. These related to confessions made to Malachi Reed, Helen Callanan, Richie Shelley, and Bill Fuller. The three judges presiding over the trial believed the confessions to be real.

Malachi Reed

On 4 February 1997, Ian Bailey gave his 14-year-old neighbour, Malachi Reed, a lift home. This was a week before Bailey was first arrested. It was a common practice for neighbours to give each other lifts. Bailey confessed to Reed during the journey.

Malachi told his Mother, Miranda Reed, and they did not hesitate to tell the Gardai. Since then, and right up to the

2019 criminal trial in France, both Malachi and his mother have been unswerving in their evidence under oath.

Why would an adult who presumes to be professional and well-educated do this to a boy? A young woman had been horribly murdered, and Bailey thought such an outburst was acceptable. Unless, of course, the horrendous nature of his crime was disturbing Bailey's mind. Or he wanted the 'joy' of speaking about his crime while maximising deniability.

Helen Callanan

Hellen Callanan was an experienced professional journalist. In 1997 she was news editor at the Sunday Tribune. She had commissioned Bailey to cover the murder of Sophie. Bailey's confession did not amuse Callanan. She did not consider Bailey to be joking and did not misunderstand Bailey's tone or delivery. She asked him the question about him being a suspect, as was said in journalistic circles. It was an important question because it would be unacceptable for a suspect to cover the murder he may have committed. As a journalist, he would have access to information not afforded to others. He could also write misleading articles pushing narratives that may interfere with the investigation of the case.

Richie Shelley

On New Year's Eve 1998, Ian Bailey and Jules Thomas invited the Shelleys to their home for drinks. The conversation was turned relentlessly to the murder of Sophie Toscan du

Plantier. Bailey had many press cuttings on the case. The Shelleys were in no doubt that Bailey confessed to the murder. They rejected any suggestion that this was 'the drink talking.' The couple were frightened by these events, and they left shortly afterward. Like many other people who were subjected to Bailey's confessions, they informed the Gards.

Bill Fuller

The other confession mentioned in the French Court's judgment was made to Bill Fuller. It is reproduced in the box below.

Fuller was a friend and occasional employer of Ian Bailey. He visited him to tell him that there were rumours in the locality that he was the murderer. In a bizarre outburst, Bailey accused Fuller of being the murderer, saying:

> "It was you who did it. You saw her at spar and she excited you walking in the alleys with her tight bottom so you went to her house to see what you could get from her but she wasn't interested, you attacked her, she ran and you followed her and you threw something at the back of her head and you went too far, much further than you had intended to."

Fuller was certain that Bailey was telling him how he, Bailey, had murdered Sophie. He made this clear when giving evidence in the Bailey trial in 2019. Other evidence supports Fuller's conclusion. First, the brutal attack on the head from behind was not widely known outside the investigating officers. Second, at the French trial, a clinical psychologist explained that this type of confession enables the perpetrator to project his negative feelings and actions onto others.

A third source of support comes from further comments made by Bailey during this episode. He said that seeing and pursuing Sophie resembles the way he became involved with Jules Thomas. In his confession, Bailey refers to Fuller as 'seeing Sophie in Spar.' After first denying that he saw Sophie in the shops in Schull on December 21st, 1996 (a lie), he later admitted it. The shops in this area included the Spar, and Sophie did visit the shop that day. Bailey refers to such a visit while claiming he did not know what she looked like.

2019 Court conclusion

The trial judges concluded that on three separate occasions, and with people with whom Bailey was a neighbour, professional colleague or friend, he admitted being the perpetrator of the murder. With a fourth person, he gave a detailed description of the nature of the aggressive attack on Sophie. This description was provided to the friend in the form of suggesting he had committed the crime. The confessions described in the judgment were sometimes when Bailey was sober, sometimes after he had been drinking.

The judges rejected the suggestion that Bailey's confessions were attributable to him being sarcastic or ironic. They pointed out that Bailey knew he was a suspect when he made the comments, and he was in no doubt about the severity of the case nor the inappropriateness of making jokes about such a death. The judges noted that all the witnesses believed the confessions were serious and true. They all cut off contact with Bailey and promptly reported their concerns to An Garda Siochana.

The further confessions

While the French court focused on the four confessions above, Ian Bailey made many more. In the DPP report of 2001, five confessions were scrutinised. These are from Ungerer, Callanan, Reed, McKenna, and the Shelleys. In part three, the DPP analysis of those confessions will be reviewed. The analysis was poor. Anyone believing the DPP and the French court must have covered all the confession evidence may be surprised to learn that there were at least twelve confessions witnessed by eighteen people. Some confessions were made in the presence of more than one person.

A list of the confessions

Witnesses	Cumulative witnesses	Confessions
M Reed	1	1
H Callanan	2	2
R. Shelley + Shelley	4	3
B Fuller	5	4
Y Ungerer	6	5
B Hogan	7	6

Grant + Penney+ O'Colmain	10	7
J Mckenna	11	8
C Mangèz	12	9
Fuller M + Fuller B senior	14	10
Barrett + Deady + Graham	17	11
K Hendricks	18	12

The other confessions

Yvonne Ungerer

The day following his first arrest, Ian Bailey telephoned Yvonne Ungerer at approximately 12 to 12.30 pm. He told her that he and Thomas had been arrested regarding the murder of Sophie Toscan du Plantier. In her statement made to the police on the day of the call she said: " I then asked him what happened? Why did they arrest you? And he replied that some witnesses who had seen him down by the water or causeway had come forward. I asked him what time it was, and he said that it was early in the morning. I think he said around 4 a.m." she added, " ....He did not say whether he was walking or driving or specify where exactly the water or causeway was. I said what were you doing there, and he said, "Oh, I suppose I was washing the blood off my clothes. I felt he said that in a half-joking way. "

In a later statement Ungerer reported a conversation she had with Bailey. She stated to the Police: "At some point during this conversation, I asked Ian about this sighting of him during the night as I had spoken of in my last statement. I asked him what were you doing in your car down at the Causeway and he replied, "No, no there was no car", he didn't really elaborate on that."

Bill Hogan

While working on stories, Ian Bailey spoke to Bill Hogan. Bailey knew that Hogan was a local cheese maker, and Sophie was a regular customer, so they got to know each other well. Michael Sheridan, the author of outstanding books on the case, tells us that Hogan knew Sophie to be a cultured, decent, and modest person.

At one point, Bailey sells a story to the Sunday Tribune, claiming that Sophie would get a divorce. The story is attributed to a 'local cheesemaker.' Hogan said no such thing, it was a fabrication. When confronted about this, Bailey said it was part of a ploy to flush out the 'real murderer.' A member of the Corsican mafia 'hired by Sophie's husband.' Despite this, Hogan offered to help Bailey meet people he knew in France and even offered to pay for his flight.

Bailey's final visit to Bill Hogan was in early to mid-January. He told Hogan he could not visit France as he was a murder suspect. Bailey was perturbed and emotional. He explained that he could not remember anything about the night of the murder, suggesting that he may need hypnosis to help him remember. Bailey says, 'I will go down for mental….just like that guy in Sligo.'

His Sligo reference was to a high-profile murder case in Ireland. A man had murdered his ex-girlfriend and her mother. He was diagnosed as being insane and sent to a psychiatric facility rather than a prison. The murderer was released when deemed sane. To Bill Hogan, this was Bailey considering an insanity plea for the murder of Sophie. Hogan promptly got Bailey out of his home and never welcomed him there again.

The birthday party

In February 1997, Ian Bailey attended a birthday party. There, he was asked why he had murdered Sophie. According to Paul Grant, in a statement made in August 1997, Bailey answered "'I did it to resurrect my journalistic career". Grant explained that he had not taken a drink then, and Bailey was not drunk. After making the comment, Bailey exited the room quickly. In a statement given in January 1999, Ronnie Penney explained that he had been at the party and had heard Bailey's reply to the question. He said, "I did it to further my career". Penney was shocked and taken aback adding 'he appeared serious. It was not a joking comment.' Penney said some of those present left in disgust.

A third statement regarding the party was provided by Paul O'Colmain in September 1999. He said that Bailey's answer was ' to boost my career.' O'Colmain assumed Bailey was joking but added he thought it was in bad taste and inappropriate. There is a high level of agreement on what Bailey said. Two people believed it was a real confession, and one thought it was an unpleasant 'joke.'

Galley Inn

James McKenna and Diane McKenna gave statements to AGS on 21.04.1997 and 28.04.1997, respectively. They described a trip from Co. Down to Schull on April 8th earlier that month. There, they met Ian Bailey and Jules Thomas at the Galley Inn. During their time together, Bailey confessed to the murder.

They sat close to Bailey and Thomas and started talking to each other. Thomas said she was an artist, and Bailey said he was a journalist working for the Cork Examiner. While Thomas and Mrs McKenna were talking Mr McKenna asked Bailey if he could write a poem for his wife as their wedding anniversary was coming up. Bailey asked McKenna if he knew about the murder. He had as it was on the television news in Northern Ireland. With a smirk, Bailey said, "That is me." Bailey appeared to get a kick out of saying it. From then on, Mr McKenna gave him the cold shoulder. So disturbed was McKenna that, despite him being on a holiday break, he went to the local Garda station that evening, but it was closed. He returned to the station the next day. His wife did not hear the conversation but reported that her husband had told her what Bailey said.

The flower show

In a statement made on 28/04/2002, artist Keith Hendrick told the investigators that he got to know Jules Thomas through their work as artists. Then via Thomas, he met Ian

Bailey. He learned from Bailey that he had been a journalist working on the Sophie Toscan du Plantier case. Bailey told Hendrick he had been at the scene of the crime on the day of the murder, and he had been allowed to 'trample around the site.'

In a later conversation at a local Flower show, he asked Bailey about his time at the scene of the crime. Hendrick told Bailey that in the USA, returning to the scene with cuts on his hands would result in him being immediately arrested, handcuffed, and ultimately swabbed. His reply was, "Well, Keith, if that had happened, I might not be here now talking to you." Hendrick was in no doubt this was a confession.

A French journalist

On the 8th of July 1997, Caroline Mangèz gave a statement. She was a journalist reporting on the murder for Paris Match. She covered the case extensively. She would go on to be the editor of the publication. Through her work, she got to know Ian Bailey. She stated: He told me," I could have done this to relaunch my journalistic career." There is no understanding why Bailey would find his comments appropriate or even remotely funny. Mangèz did not interpret his comments as sarcastic or ironic.

At the artist's home

After his release following his first arrest, Bailey stayed at the home of artist Russell Barrett rather than go to the Prairie.

He spoke to Bailey about his arrest experience. During the conversation, he explained that the Gardai said he had a blackout, and if that is the case, He must have done it, meaning the murder. There is no record of that point being put to him in any of the interviews that took place during his interrogation. At one point, he started to cry and stated that if what the Gardai said was true, he must have done it. Barrett believed Bailey was cracking up and told him to stop.

Two other people were staying at the Barrett home. Colin Deady had a room at the house and knew Bailey from earlier in the year. Bailey had stopped there after a vicious assault on Jules Thomas. On the post-arrest stay at the house, he had heard Bailey saying that if what the Police had said about him drinking and blacking out was true, then he must have murdered Sophie. A man named Martin Graham was also present when Bailey referred to the story of the blackout, the murder, and getting a hypnotist for help. Graham also recalls that Bailey told him he had seen Sophie shopping. That final point from Graham supports the contention that Bailey knew Sophie. This issue will be explored in the next chapter.

All three men heard this tale of a blackout and Bailey 'admitting' that he might have murdered her while experiencing some strange mental fugue. Yet, there is no evidence this narrative was put to Bailey. Furthermore, Bailey gave the investigators a full account of his time. There was no scope for him 'to lose' two or more hours. A time in which he would likely be muddied and bloodied. There was no evidence, according to Bailey, that he could have committed the murder; despite this, he was keen to propagate a psychological defence – excuse?- for the murder.

This is not the only time Bailey uses a mental impairment defence. The same was done with Bill Hogan. At that time, he produced a more elaborate tale. The same heightened emotional state was followed by claims that he was not controlling himself. This is not irony or sarcasm, nor a bit of the drink talking, nor Bailey being misheard. It is a man offering an excuse for a brutal murder. Perhaps one should consider it a new version of his blaming his savage attack on Jules Thomas on ' the drink.' A typical case of Bailey refusing to take responsibility for his actions.

The confession these three men heard was not Bailey's only confession on this day. Earlier in this chapter, the confession heard by Yvonne Ungerer was described. Both these confessions came the day after Bailey had been challenged about his role in the murder

It is worth noting here that later, Bailey loved to spread the story that on the way to the police station after his first arrest, the officers threatened him with violence. He says they told him he could end up dead. He continued to push that narrative in his risible podcast. However, that matter did not come up in his conversations with Barrett, Deady, Graham, or other people immediately after his interrogation. He was crying and emotional but said nothing of the alleged death threats. Bailey spoke of blackouts and finding a hypnotist but did not comment on AGS death threats. Most likely, they never happened.

Mary Fuller and Bill Fuller senior

Statements were made on July 1st 1997, by Mary Fuller and Bill Fuller senior. She explained how Ian Bailey showed her a newspaper article that said a local man had been picked up by Police in connection with Sophie's murder. As she read the paper, Mrs Fuller heard Bailey say, "I did it, and she helped me; that's what they are saying." The article was a general piece and did not refer to the man's identity. Jules Thomas was present and said nothing. Mary Fuller was adamant that Bailey was not joking or laughing. She had met Bailey several times, so she knew his moods. To her, he was serious, and he had not been drinking.

He then stood up and said, "I did it, and he pointed to Jules, who helped me. That's what "they" were saying. I asked what he meant by "they," and he said the locals and the Gardai. I thought his remark was quite strange, strange enough to remember."

A summary of the confessions

The cases summarised herewith are more than sufficient for the reader to judge what Bailey did and said. Bailey denies all the statements saying he confessed. He denies a few ever happened. For the rest, he claims people misheard him or lied or failed to appreciate his 'subtle' sense of humour. We know for sure that Bailey repeatedly lies. There is no evidence that the eighteen witnesses to the twelve confessions were lying or had any incentive to do so. Nor is there evidence to suggest they were hard of hearing or could not detect ironic speech. They had no ulterior motives to mislead investigators.

In four of the confessions, multiple witnesses corroborated each other. In another, Mr. McKenna immediately told his wife what he had heard. Of the remaining confessions, two were made to experienced journalists. The confessions were done in different ways to a broad cross-section of people. The Barrett and Hogan statements have Bailey exploring the idea that he murdered Sophie due to an unnatural psychological state.

The Bill Fuller confession has a lot of detail about how the murder happened. It also refers to 'Fuller' seeing Sophie in the shop. This is interesting because Graham stated that Bailey said he had seen Sophie shopping. Only a man who knew what Sophie looked like could make such an assertion. This slip shows he knew more about Sophie than he admitted. The confessions of Ungerer and to Barrett, Deedy and Graham were made on the same day.

When some of these witnesses gave evidence in civil proceedings, they were seen as being far more credible than Bailey. We should not forget that Bailey lost in two civil trials. He was humiliated in the witness box and by the verdicts of a Judge and a Jury.

Ian Bailey sought to discredit these witnesses, and the DPP bought the snake oil he was selling. As we will see, the DPP analysis of the confession evidence was limited, questionable, and fell below what the family of any murder victim should expect.

We have a choice. Was Bailey making ironic jokes about a woman recently murdered in a horrific fashion while all the other people had no sense of humour or were 'too stupid' to get Bailey's clever jokes? Or could it be that eighteen people were hearing the confessions of a narcissist desperate to say what he had done?

In Ireland, the DPP appeared strongly inclined to agree with Bailey rather than the 5 independent witnesses they reviewed. Yet when many of these witnesses—along with many others—presented evidence to the courts, they were credible and believable.

There is no suggestion that the eighteen witnesses had major psychiatric disorders or were under the influence of psychotropic drugs. Nor is there any reason to believe these people conspired to incriminate Ian Bailey. There is every indication that they were normal people disturbed by the confessions and convinced Bailey meant them.

In these cases, a Jury or Judge has to decide who they believe. Maybe every single one of these witnesses has produced a series of lies about Ian Bailey. More likely, Bailey confessed, as many murderers do.

If just one confession is correct, he has admitted he did it

For statements, see Appendix 2: pt 9

CHAPTER 9

Bailey knew Sophie

One of the most frequently debated topics has been how well Ian Bailey knew Sophie Toscan du Plantier. He always claimed that before her death, he had only seen her once. That occurred when he was doing some labouring work for the neighbours of Sophie. These were Alfie Lyons and his partner Shirley Foster. It would be Foster who would discover the deceased woman on December 23rd, 1996. Bailey says that while working for Lyons in the summer of 1995, he 'saw' Sophie up to 100 metres away. Lyons allegedly pointed her out to Bailey. He was outside, and she was inside her cottage. With summer daylight looking up an incline, Bailey would not have had a clear view of Sophie.

In his many interviews after the murder, Bailey repeated this version of events. The key point was that he did not know what she looked like. He also claimed Lyons told him only that the woman was French.

He must also have been told by someone that it was a holiday home, as he later stated this was so. He made no mention of Lyons telling him this. It is rather strange that Lyons said she was French and nothing else when he pointed out Sophie. Not a word about her age, occupation, frequency of visits, friendliness, or otherwise. Nothing. One is also to believe that Bailey did not ask Alfie any questions about her. It is hard to believe that the men had no conversation about the French cottage owner. The surprising thing here is Bailey's claim of knowing virtually nothing about this woman.

In chapter two, in the section on the deceased, Bailey reveals that he knew Sophie still owned the cottage, that she was staying alone at the cottage, that she was the dead woman, and that she had been murdered. It defies belief that he knew all that while claiming to be ignorant regarding Sophie.

Furthermore the evidence in chapters three and four could not be clearer. Bailey knew of the murder of a French woman before anyone else. He told people this and admitted to visiting the crime scene before the Gards had even put up a cordon. He knew it hours before his call from Cassidy. He admitted to knowing where the body was and to driving straight there. He went to the Post office stating the dead woman was the French cottage owner when he had not formally established the identity of the victim..Knowing all that information suggests he had a deep knowledge of Sophie.

The evidence from many witnesses is clear. Bailey knew Sophie by his actions and the knowledge he possessed.

We know because he told us

There are many other reasons to believe that Bailey knew Sophie. The source of these many reasons is Ian Bailey. He told over a dozen people that he knew her. These admissions that he knew Sophie are recorded in statements taken by investigating officers.

British journalist Paul Webster said Ian Bailey indicated that he knew Sophie. Webster was working for the Observer. He was also working for the Guardian during 1996 and 1997. He was based in Paris. After the murder, Webster was contacted by Bailey, who claimed he was in a good position to provide information. Webster said, "He made it absolutely clear that he had talked to her - before, there is no doubt about that at all - and seen her on the day she died," In his statement to investigators (27/03/1997) Webster said the following "In the course of a conversation, in which I took only brief and easily legible notes, he told me that he knew Sophie Toscan du Plantier and had met and talked with her several times. At the time I had no idea that Bailey was a suspect and I did not press him for details". This could not be clearer from a reputable journalist. Bailey said he knew Sophie.

The evidence of Webster also confirms statements from other people. He is clear Bailey said he saw Sophie on the day she died. This is what Bailey later told the investigators. He also alluded to it when 'accusing' Bill Fuller of murdering Sophie. He gave Martin Graham a similar story. He knew who she was and told four different people he saw her on the 22nd.

A second journalist, Helen Callanan, the News editor for the Sunday Tribune, made a statement on 10.02.1997 concerning Bailey. She told investigators, "Every week since then (Sophie's murder), we would talk on a Thursday or a Friday to see if there was an update on theory. During these weeks he had told me that he had been questioned by the

Gardai and that he had spoken to Sophie before she was murdered, that is that he had met her before." The question for anyone deciding whether Bailey was culpable is whether they believe Bailey or Webster and Callanan.

This is not the only time this question must be posed. It comes up several times. Does one believe Webster and Callanan regarding Bailey knowing Sophie? Are Tribune journalists Curran and McEnaney to be believed when they say they had no contact with Bailey on the morning of the 23rd and the article was submitted late.? Likewise, there is a choice to be made between Cross and McSweeney, on the one hand, and Bailey, on the other, with reference to him being in Dreenane early on December 23rd.

There were many more examples indicating Bailey knew Sophie. Alfie Lyons (22.05.97) told investigators that he was pretty sure that he did more than point out Sophie from afar. He explained that Bailey had been doing some work for him for several days in June 1995. He stated: " I have a recollection of Sophie calling up to me and I introducing Ian to her but I cannot swear it." Interestingly, Lyons readily refers to Sophie by name, but Bailey insists he was never told her name. Lyons says he could not swear to introducing Bailey to Sophie. However, his assertion receives some support from Bailey himself.

Yvonne Ungerer informed the investigators, in her 22.10.1997 statement, that Bailey told her that he knew Sophie. He said he met her when he was working for Alfie Lyons. She said " I asked him again about knowing Sophie and where she lived and again he reiterated that he knew her from being at Alfie's." Thus, Alfie said he thought he had introduced Bailey to Sophie, and Bailey told Ungerer he had been introduced to Sophie by Alfie. Who to believe? Lyons and Ungerer or Bailey.

On 07.02.1997, Delia Jackson told investigators that when talking with Bailey, the subject of the murder of Sophie came up. Bailey told her that he had met Sophie on a couple of occasions. This may have stayed in Jackson's mind because she added that he was the only person she knew who had met Sophie.

> "On Christmas Day 1996, Ian Bailey called to our house. He was looking for washing up liquid and a toilet roll. I parcelled both of these and gave them to him. While he was in the house we had a general conversation and the murder of Sophie came into it. He stated that he had met Sophie on a couple of occasions. He was the only person that I met that knew Sophie."

Padraig Beirne was the photographic editor for the Irish Independent. In a statement made on 21.05.97 he said he received a telephone call from Ian Bailey, he said:

> "Mr. Bailey told me the body of a woman had been found dead in West Cork. He knew the woman was a French native. He said he had a picture of her and asked me was I interested in getting it for publication in the Irish Independent. As far as I recollect I asked him how he had the picture of her and he replied that he had taken it himself and that she was a very good looking woman (pick-up picture)."

In this case, Bailey is saying he has a photograph of Sophie. He is saying she was a French native. This is not a promise that he would get such a photograph. Bailey says he had the photograph. A newspaperman would know that the Irish media would be sending plenty of journalists and photographers to Dreenane. He said he took the photograph. This means that he knew exactly what Sophie looked like. If the photograph was taken surreptitiously then that suggests something rather improper and sleazy but also that he knew the photograph was of Sophie, so he knew her name and knew her by sight. If the photo was taken with Sophie's consent, then it is hard to imagine that this would not have been done without some conversation between the two of them. Once again, he must have known what she looked like and her name.

Bailey also volunteered that Sophie was good-looking. He was not alone in that opinion, but it indicates that he had looked closely at her and judged her attractive. This suggests that the photograph showed Sophie to be attractive. This could not have been taken at the crime scene, where taking a pleasant photo would have been impossible. The photograph must have been taken at some other time. He had engaged with Sophie on at least one other occasion and lied about only ever seeing her once in the distance.

Beirne was a successful photographic professional. He knew the difference between someone saying they had photos and describing the content of the photo and someone saying they could take photos at some time in the future.

Another photojournalist was Mike Brown, a photographer for Reuters International. He spoke to Bailey about Sophie.

He replied that he knew her by sight but did not know her socially, adding that he thought Bailey knew her name. This goes with a statement from a journalist taken on 24.02.1997. John Keirans stated that Bailey told him Alfie Lyons had told him who she was. Not only does the Keirans statement corroborate Brown's statement, but it also lends support to Lyons and Ungerer's statements.

Shortly after the murder of Sophie, Irish television was filming a reconstruction of events for a television appeal. Anne Cahalane was a local woman who resembled Sophie and appeared as Sophie in the reconstruction. Calahane was there with her partner Peter Wilson. It was mid-January 1997, and they were filming a section of the programme at Three Castles Head, a place visited by Sophie the weekend before she was murdered.

While at the location, Calahane and Wilson were approached by Ian Bailey. He told them that he was a journalist covering the murder and he had met Sophie Toscan du Plantier. He also told them that he had met Sophie on the walk to Three Castles Head. Cahalane read a newspaper article in 2012 in which Bailey had said he did not know Sophie. Peter Wilson told investigators Bailey told them he met Sophie on the walk and that he knew her. Calahane repeated this information under oath in Bailey's failed civil action against AGS.

A local arts and crafts worker gave a statement 24/25.02.1997. Irma Tullock said Bailey told her he had met the French woman sometime in the past. He did not refer to seeing her in the distance but that he had met her. Colin

Deady was staying at the home of Russell Barratt when Bailey went there following his first arrest. He told investigators that Bailey told him he knew the lady who had been murdered. Martin Graham made a statement on 18.02.1997. He was also at the Barrett home at the same time as Deady and he said Bailey told him he knew the murdered 'girl'.

For statements, see Appendix 2: pt 10

The growing evidence against Bailey

In his 31.12.1996 statement, Ian Bailey gave the investigators a false alibi. He lied about where he was and what he was doing at the time Sophie died. He was also unequivocal in saying he knew exactly where he would find the deceased woman and that he drove straight to the crime scene. These two key statements illustrate important patterns of Ian Bailey's behaviour that were to be seen many times in the years to come.

The false alibi is a typical Bailey bare-faced lie. He is in some form of trouble, this time extremely serious trouble, so he tells a lie and hopes to brazen it out. When one of his lies is exposed or he believes it is about to be exposed, he will change his story. Often replacing one lie with another. At other times, when Bailey realised that a truth that he thought insignificant was actually damaging, he would slip into lying mode. He will obfuscate and create false narratives. He will then embellish his false narrative, believing that will make it more plausible.

In the world Bailey grew up in, he could get away with these patterns. However, a murder case made the stakes infinitely higher. Furthermore, everything was recorded. Denial and lies are much easier to get away with when things are not recorded. The taking of written statements, trial testimony, social media output, articles by Bailey, recorded interviews, and podcasts featuring him created a record of his many falsehoods and lies. It was not a case of him remembering or forgetting what happened. It was about him being unable to recall all the lies he had told. He drowned in his own lies.

The chapters in part one of this book reveal a man endlessly lying in an attempt to hide the truth. Once that is understood, it demands that anything Bailey said in life, and in particular concerning the case, could not be taken at face value.

As the focus shifts from Bailey's 'Billy liar' narratives it was possible to move inexorably closer to the truth. In chapter three, the evidence from a variety of people showed what Bailey actually knew from very early morning on 23.12.96, that a French woman who owned a holiday cottage in Dreenane had been murdered there. Further evidence showed that Bailey drove to the hidden scene of the crime, and he knew the dead woman was the cottage owner. This evidence came from almost twenty people. These people could not know how their inputs when combined with all the others would make such a compelling case against Bailey.

In part two there is substantial circumstantial evidence supporting what was found in part one. The chaotic and contradictory statements made by Bailey and the Thomas family about turkeys, a tree, and injuries are shambolic. The five witnesses manage to offer over ten contradictory versions of what happened. There were significant variations in their stories in terms of what was done, when it was done, who did it, and the injuries allegedly suffered by Bailey. This is in stark contrast with the statements from the people who last saw Bailey prior to the murder. Seven people reported no injuries at all to hands, arms, and head. Something happened after Bailey left the Galley bar to cause readily noticeable scratches to his hands and arms and a cut to his head.

A confession to one or two people is rare. A man who confessed at least twelve times in front of eighteen witnesses appears to be unprecedented. Bailey was sometimes sober, sometimes drunk; He was at times distressed and emotional while at others apparently enjoying his confessions. The people hearing him were not the socially challenged fools that Bailey would have people believe. They know what they heard and they reported it. The nature of the confessions varied but the core content was the same. A judge who heard some of these witnesses under cross-examination had no difficulty believing them. Ian Bailey repeatedly confessed to the murder.

There are many reasons to conclude Ian Bailey knew Sophie. At the time of the murder, he knew a lot about the victim and where she could be found. He also told many people that he knew her. He told this to journalists, friends, and casual acquaintances. Despite his claims that he did not know Sophie, his words and deeds indicate otherwise.

This evidence leads us to one conclusion. Ian Bailey murdered Sophie Toscan du Plantier. The conclusion leads to one question: Why wasn't Bailey charged for the murder? In part three the question will be answered.

Notes

Following the Bailey versions of events proferred in 1996 and 1998 and presented in Chapter 2, it is now possible to offer a third description of what happened, One that draws upon dozens of corroborating statements rather than Bailey's lies.

> **The version of events based on dozens of corroborated statements**
>
> **On the evening of December 21st and the morning of the 22nd**
>
> Bailey lied about where he was the night of the 21st and the morning of the 22nd. It is unknown why he did so.
>
> **The evening of the 22nd**
>
> One witness in the Galley bar made reference to some markings on one of Bailey's hands. Seven witnesses saw no injuries to Bailey's head, hands, and arms. The injuries Bailey had from the 23rd onwards were not witnessed in the bar
>
> The only sources of the narrative for the journey home that night are Bailey and Thomas. Bailey was a pathological liar, and Thomas changed her story on more than one issue about what happened at this time. It is possible to conclude that false narratives were presented. Bailey chose to lie about going to Hunt's Hill and looking towards Dreenane.

The morning of the 23rd

After Bailey's false alibi was exposed he offered many false narratives for what he claimed to be doing that morning. However, the statements from dozens of witnesses make it clear.

Bailey and Thomas left the cottage between 9 am and 10 am, Bailey told two people he was at the scene of the crime sometime around 10.30 am and before any cordon was put in place. He knew about the murder when he left the Prairie.

Thomas went to do some shopping and told James Camier that there was a murdered French woman in Dreenane and that Bailey was there on behalf of a newspaper. By noon Thomas told her daughter about the death,

All these events show the pair knew about the murder from early morning.

Furthermore, there was no record that Bailey called the Tribune that morning, nor did Bailey or Thomas answer the phone when the Tribune called the Prairie.

Two further statements were given saying Bailey, around noon, said he was working as a journalist on the case of a murdered Frenchwoman in the Toormore area.

On the 23rd, Bailey was sporting injuries that had not been seen in the Galley bar the previous night.

The call and the following eighty minutes

It was shown that Bailey knew all about the murder of Sophie many hours before the call from Eddie Cassidy at 1.40 pm. He knew who the victim was and where she could be found.

Bailey initially lied, saying he was told the deceased was French. In 1998, he conceded that he had given false statements on nationality. Furthermore, Cassidy was adamant that he made no mention of nationality to Bailey or anyone else when he called people about the death. Fenella Thomas supported Cassidy, saying that after he received the call, Bailey made no reference to the deceased being French.

Bailey did know exactly where to find the scene of the crime and he drove straight there.[He later lied to cover up that he knew, but no one was being conned]. He did not need to ask questions because he knew where he was going and what he would find.

The early statements of Bailey, his own actions, and the statements of Thomas and Foster confirmed that he knew where to go.

On leaving Dreenane, Bailey drove to the Post office and specifically asked for the name of the French cottage owner, the deceased. This version was corroborated by Thomas. Dukelow and Jermyn. He knew the dead woman was the cottage owner. He almost certainly knew her name but went through the charade of pretending that he needed to get it.

Confessions

In the weeks immediately following the murder, Bailey confessed many times.

PART THREE
A Betrayal of Justice?

Introduction - The analysis of the DPP Report 2001

Ian Bailey was not charged and sent to trial because the Office of the Director of Public Prosecutions (DPP) decided, 'The evidence does not warrant a prosecution against Bailey.' This was the conclusion of a controversial report written in 2001 by Robert Sheehan, a lawyer employed by the DPP. The report was supported by three DPP directors: Eamon Barnes, James Hamilton, and Clare Loftus. In the following chapters, the report will be scrutinised in considerable detail. It builds upon the excellent analysis done by Elio Malocco in his book Killing Sophie.

The Garda investigation at the time of the 2001 report was over 2000 pages in length, while the French file in 2019 was over 2400 pages. One of the most startling aspects of the DPP report [Analysis of the evidence to link Ian Bailey to the Sophie Toscan du Plantier murder] was its brevity. It was only 44 pages. This was exceptionally brief, and as we will see, it resulted in many startling omissions.

For decades, Ian Bailey affirmed that the DPP report confirmed his innocence. This was and remains a dishonest assertion. Even if one accepted the report's recommendation that Bailey should not be charged, that does not comment on whether he is ultimately guilty or innocent. Ian Bailey had scant regard for the truth and lied with impunity..

Bailey used the DPP report as the cornerstone of arguments in many legal cases. Each time he lost. His libel case against national newspapers failed miserably in the Irish Circuit Court, leaving him with substantial debts. In that case, Counsel for the newspapers, Paul Gallagher, addressed Bailey's continuous lies regarding the murder of Sophie Toscan du Plantier. This sharply contrasted with the DPP report, which made little or no references to Bailey's prolific lying. Furthermore, witnesses ignored or dismissed by the DPP were found plausible and convincing by the judge, Patrick Moran.

The High Court case in 2014 to 2015

The High Court case in which Ian Bailey Jules Thomas and Marie Farrell sought to sue the Garda Commissioner and the State ran for over sixty days. The DPP report, its author, and other DPP figures were prominent during the trial.

The High Court judge presiding over the case, Mr Justice Hedigan, refused to allow the DPP report to be entered into evidence. On more than one occasion, the Judge admonished the author of the report, Robert Sheehan, for his conduct. He believed that Sheehan was voicing his opinions rather than presenting facts. Regarding Sheehan's language, the Judge said it was: "completely inappropriate for a public servant to be giving, somebody who worked in the DPP's office." The judge wanted counsel to control the witness as he ignored court rules. Justice Hedigan added, "If I do form the impression and I already do have concerns

Introduction - The analysis of the DPP Report 2001

about this matter that there is a high level of unfairness developing in relation to this matter, I will discharge the jury, I don't want to do that but unless I can get a decision from this jury that is entirely fair and made in accordance with the evidence then I don't think they should be allowed to continue to a verdict at all, " That a judge considered stopping a high-profile and resource-intensive trial is an indication of just how much he thought the trial might be being compromised.

The jury needed only a couple of hours to deliver a crushing defeat to Bailey. His civil case against AGS had failed. It left him millions of euros in debt. A debt he made no effort to address while continuing to get drunk, smoke, run a car, and take drugs at the expense of the Irish people.

The 2001 report

The decision not to prosecute Bailey is astonishing in light of all that was known at the time. However, there is an important caveat here. Anyone reading the report and nothing else may be minded to agree with the author, Robert Sheehan, and all the DPP apparatchiks. The conclusions may have some validity if the report had got it even remotely right. It did not.

The two dominant conclusions reached by the DPP were (1) there were no grounds for charging Bailey and (2) AGS behaved in a way that may, in some circles, be deemed wholly inappropriate. However, the report cannot be taken at face value.

Some smaller concerns

The short and poorly referenced DPP document contains both minor and major concerns. All of them raise as yet unanswered questions about the report's validity.

On occasions, irrelevant information finds its way into the report. For example, the report dedicates a paragraph to one of Ian Bailey's preposterous theories of the crime. This distractor was the suggestion that a French lover of Sophie may be guilty of the murder. Bailey had written about this without providing evidence. This will be addressed in chapter 12.

In addition to inappropriate information, there is also inaccurate information. The most unforgivable example in the 2001 report occurred when the report was wrong on the time the body was found and the name of the person who found the deceased. These are dreadful errors. It is unknown whether senior DPP staff apologised for these failings.

Sheehan repeatedly stated Jules Thomas was not lawfully arrested (wrong) and claim that statements not made soon after a crime cannot be relied upon (wrong again)

These sorts of things should not be found in an important legal document. They make no contribution to the issue at hand and create the impression that the report is unreliable and unprofessional. Yet that is how the report ended up, fully accepted by the Office of the Director of Public Prosecutions. This is bad enough, but it gets worse. Indeed, it is the tip of the iceberg.

Introduction - The analysis of the DPP Report 2001

Major concerns

There are significant problems with the 2001 report. They are so bad that they ought to render the document unfit for purpose. Any of these 3 issues would be enough to see the report binned immediately. To have all three defies belief. The issues are:

1. A lack of any obvious method for analysing the evidence
2. The repeated use of assumptions and inferences without sufficient or any underpinning evidence.
3. The widescale exclusions of dozens of statements that directly and indirectly demonstrate Bailey's culpability.

The 2001 report comprised 16 sections. Three sections (4. 8, and 13) somewhat surprisingly focus on the An Garda Síochána. These will be addressed in chapters 10 and 11. The DPP presents the heart of the case regarding Bailey in six sections (2, 6, 9, 10, 12 and 15). These sections will be addressed in chapters 12 to 15. The remaining sections will be found in Appendix 4.

List of the sections

1. Lack of Forensic Evidence linking Ian Bailey to the murder scene
2. Ian Bailey's alleged prior knowledge of Sophie Toscan Du Plantier.
3. Detention of Jules Thomas, allegedly on suspicion of committing the murder
4. Warnings issued by the Gardaí as to the alleged danger presented by Bailey to the community.

5. Premonition.
6. Inconsistencies in relation to Bailey's response to Garda questioning.
7. Unreliability of Marie Farrell
8. Relationship between Gardaí and certain witnesses
9. Alleged informal admissions by Bailey.
10. Scratches
11. Bailey's alleged incriminating knowledge of the murder.
12. Knowledge of injuries to body of deceased.
13. Other aspects of Garda Investigation
14. Fire on the Thomas property.
15. Alleged similar fact evidence and sexual motive.
16. General

This report kept Bailey out of prison for over twenty-seven years and prevented him from having a murder trial for twenty-three years. The legal maxim 'Justice delayed is justice denied' rings true here. If the DPP got it wrong in 2001, then Sophie Toscan du Plantier and her family have been denied justice for over a quarter of a century. After reading this part of the book, you can decide whether there has been a betrayal of justice.

CHAPTER **10**

The 'prosecution' of AGS

There were three sections in the report that focused on AGS. The main premise of all of them was that AGS behaved in a way that led to Bailey being unfairly treated and potentially being unfairly 'fitted up' for the murder. This is not said clearly and directly. It is insinuated. Much time and effort went into the preparation of these sections. The first section implies that the organisation as a whole sent messages to the West Cork community that were inappropriate and damaging for Ian Bailey. In the second section, the focus shifts from the organisation to naming officers who were alleged to have put undue pressure on specific individuals. The final section is a short cobbled-together addition to the report. The first half of it is a further allegation of improper officer conduct.

If the allegations were true, they would be a cause for grave concern. One would hope they would be supported by precise, testable evidence and miscreants dealt with severely. Should the allegations be based on speculation, it raises the question: Why? What would motivate people to make unfounded allegations?

Warnings issued by the Gardaí as to the alleged danger presented by Bailey to the community (Report section 4)

This was the longest of the three sections. The DPP's accusation is spelled out in the section heading: AGS issued warnings about Ian Bailey being a danger to the community. The implication is that these warnings may have caused people to proffer false information in an attempt to frame Ian Bailey.

To make sense of what the report author was claiming, it would be worth seeing the types of warnings he refers to and specific details about who was warned. Presumably, there would be statements from some recipients. Naturally, one would expect there to be some indications of how these warnings influenced people's statements

Examples of the warnings issued by Gardai

Specifics about the community members receiving these warnings

The impact of AGS warnings on actual statements

The boxes above have no content because the DPP report provided no evidence to support the assertion that there were warnings and the warnings had some impact on the community. They are assumptions with no substance. If there needs to be no proof supporting accusations or assumptions, then anything can be suggested. In this case, with almost infinite possibilities, the DPP chooses to make these accusations against AGS. They have never explained why they did this.

It is worth looking at what was included in this report section. The opening explained that the Gardai had submitted a report to the DPP for consultation. It presented their concerns. Police officers, in good faith, and because of the evidence before them, believed that Ian Bailey posed a threat to his community. They raised it with the DPP. This is what most citizens would want from their police force. The report stated:

"the Gardaí stated the following: 6 1. It is of the utmost importance that Bailey be charged immediately with this murder as there is every possibility that he will kill again. 2. It is reasonable to suggest that witnesses living close to him are in imminent danger of attack. 3. The only way to prevent a further attack or killing is to take Bailey into custody on a charge of murder and this point cannot be over-stressed."

This appears to be a sensible issue to raise. Bailey was prone to violence and sexual inappropriateness when drunk. He was drunk many times a week. A man who, according to his diaries, had been regularly violent to Thomas during 1996. In the summer of 1996, Bailey had hospitalised Jules Thomas after a severe beating. Despite the efforts of the DPP to downplay the summer attack, it was frightful. In his diaries, he stated that he tried to kill his partner. It would have been remiss if the officers had not raised the issue with the DPP.

Then the DPP report goes on to say:

> "It is understood that the Gardaí issued similar warnings about Bailey to members of the community."

Regrettably, we are not told how the author came to such an understanding when he can produce no evidence. The report author is expected to understand what constitutes evidence but produces none to support his conclusions. He could have done so if he had wished to gather more information. Instead, assumptions are stated as facts. This is not good enough. In a case of this importance, it is not too much to ask that the author provide some actual examples of these warnings and name some of the people who received them.

The report then goes on to single out the case of Paul O'Colmain. A witness in the case and a one-time friend of Ian Bailey. The report states that O'Colmain was concerned that he was being associated with Bailey. As he had been Bailey's friend, it would have been odd if he had not been associated with him. Mr O'Colmain pointed out that he had tried to distance himself from Bailey. That is commendable and something that people may do when a neighbour, known to be violent, is arrested for a brutal murder. Moreover, O'Colmain had given a statement saying that Bailey told him about the murder of Sophie around noon on December 23rd. Bailey denied O'Colmain's statement and implied he was lying. It is little wonder O'Colmain would put distance between himself and the alleged murderer.

O'Colmain's solicitor wrote to the Gardai to deny any ongoing association with Bailey. There is nothing here about warnings made to the community. It is an empty narrative. However, the author draws an inference from his own fact-free proposition.

> "By inference, it seems that the O'Colmains are afraid that if they align themselves with Ian Bailey on any matter they will incur the disapproval of the Gardaí."

Where does that inference come from? Not one bit of evidence is presented to show O'Colmain was warned, which means there is no known content of such warnings available. This is all smoke and mirrors. It has no place in a report of this importance. Nor is there any evidence of fear — none. The author resorts to this mind reading and emotion reading several times in the report. This wild speculation should not be mistaken for evidence. Regrettably, the report fails to inform the readers about the potentially large number of people who never had communications with AGS but still wanted no alignment or contact with Bailey.

The report adds that cannabis was found at the O'Colmain home, and the son had a drug habit. This does not mean there is any evidence of warnings. This statement of fact morphs into the following assumptions and conclusions.

> "It might, for this reason, be thought that the unfortunate O'Colmains under such circumstances are most anxious to ingratiate themselves with the Gardaí and as such are witnesses of very little weight."

A summary of what actually happened with the O'Colmain family is in the table below

Implied behaviour	Evidence
O'Colmain gave false evidence / withheld true evidence,	NONE
O'Colmain was pressured by AGS to provide 'helpful evidence'	NONE
O'Colmain received any messages from AGS that put pressure on him	NONE
There is clear factual evidence showing that O'Colmain's statements have very little weight	NONE

The whole narrative generated here is fact-free. The anti-AGS narrative undermines a witness who gave evidence detrimental to Bailey. Why would this false narrative be created, and why would it end up in the 2001 report? These are questions that have not been answered.

The report refers to Bill Fuller and explains some events in his life around the time of the crime. However, there is a complete absence of evidence relating to the subject of this section, namely that the Gardai issued warnings regarding Bailey's danger to the community. This is preposterous.

The report states, 'There has been a consistent flow of information to the media concerning the investigation." And so there should be. A high-profile international murder should have extensive media coverage, and investigators should work with the media. If there was evidence that officers were inappropriately briefing the press against Bailey, the report should have presented it. This did not happen. There seems to be nothing but speculation.

Much of this section, approximately 40%, is a regurgitation of a story told by Ian Bailey to a journalist. They are the opinions of Ian Bailey. At no time does the report refer to his comments as allegations. Bailey is playing the victim. The report does not explain that playing the victim is a common ploy among criminals. Despite all the complaints by Bailey, there was not a single piece of independent evidence supporting the assertion that the Gardai warned people about him. Let's take a closer look at the interview.

This recorded interview is presented on over 1.5 pages of a 44-page report. It is presented uncritically and accounts for almost half of the section about warnings.

In the first point, the DPP says Bailey alleges harassment. For the remainder of this Bailey narrative, there is no further reference to his statements being allegations. This might explain why the report uses words like alleged and alleging very skewedly. The word is used over 50 times in the full report, and 90% of those times, it concerned evidence indicating Bailey's guilt. It is only used a handful of times with reference to evidence supporting Bailey.

Excerpts from the DPP report	The evidence the DPP provides regarding warnings
The tape recording made by Caroline Mangez primarily relates to conversations with Ian Bailey recorded on or about 14 February 1997. A conversation recorded some five months later is also to be heard. The recordings are significantly different in tone and content to the statement made by Caroline Mangèz to the Gardaí. By way of stark contrast she is clearly at ease with Bailey on tape. The part of the tape which would appear to have been recorded on 14 February 1997 includes the following:	No evidence of warnings by AGS
1. Bailey alleging that he has been hounded, harassed and demonised. He states that he had nothing to do with the killing.	One of the rare times something in support of Bailey is said to be an allegation. Bailey provides zero evidence. It is his opinion. However, the DPP fails to question the utterances of a proven liar. No evidence of warnings by AGS

2. He states that he was disorientated during detention on 10 February 1997. He alleges that between ten to twelve police officers questioned him during the detention. He asserts that Gda. J.P. Culligan was aggressive, particularly during the journey from his home to the Garda Station.	There is no evidence to corroborate his story. It is purely a Bailey narrative. On the 11th, Bailey went to Russell Barratt's home, where several people were staying. Bailey mentioned none of this to Barratt, Deady, or Graham, who all made statements. Nor did he mention it to Ungerer on the 11th. Why does the DPP fail to put in the report that the Bailey as victim tale came several days later? **No evidence of warnings by AGS**
3. He states that the driver of the car was named "Liam" and this man told Bailey that even if the Gardaí did not pin it on him that he was finished in Ireland. Liam told him that somebody other than the Gardaí would put a bullet in the back of his head.	Exactly as for point 2 **No evidence of warnings by AGS**
4. On arrival at the Garda Station, the press and photographers were there. Bailey says that they clearly had been tipped off.	More than likely, someone had tipped off the press. Still - **No evidence of warnings by AGS**

5. Bailey asserts on tape that he is afraid that the Gardaí are determined to find evidence to convict him despite the fact that he is innocent. He again asserts that he had nothing to do with the murder and states that his conscience is clear.	Bailey had already lied several times to AGS, including giving a false alibi. **No evidence of warnings by AGS**
6. He reiterates his fear of being "stitched up" by the Gardaí.	Just because Bailey was playing the victim did not mean that the DPP had to buy his snake oil. **No evidence of warnings by AGS**
7. He states that the Gardaí were embarrassed by stories he had written which indicated that they had no idea as to who had committed the murder. He had been told this by local people.	Bailey alleges something again, but as ever, he has no evidence He was 'told' it by locals. Was it a stranger in the bar or in the street? This is ludicrous, yet it is in the report. **No evidence of warnings by AGS**
8. Bailey states that it is not unusual for him to get up during the night but on this occasion he had to get up because he had a story to write for the Sunday Tribune and it had to be submitted on Monday 23 December 1996.	Just because he states something, it does not make it so. Bailey had weeks to write the article, and he was keen to get back into journalism. Yet he waits until he is drunk and allegedly writes it around 2 a.m.–8 a.m. when it was due noon on the 23rd.

The 'prosecution' of AGS

	Bailey claims he had to get up but forgot all about this when he gave a false alibi. Despite all this, the DPP does not see anything problematic.
	No evidence of warnings by AGS
9. He states that this was a very difficult story because it was about computers and he found it difficult to write 900 words on this subject which had to refer to computer language etc. He states that he hand wrote the story in the kitchen of Jules' house and then between 7.00 and 8.00 a.m. as dawn was approaching, the first light of the day was beginning to show, he went to type it below in the studio. He says that he had to fax the story as he could not dictate it. Normally he dictates his story by telephone.	It was a story about wi-fi in West Cork. There was no need to refer to 'computer Language' This is another lie Sheehan missed!
	This report illustrated a poor grasp of basic facts, such as the Studio being 200m away from the cottage, not next door.
	If he went to type it up, he would have finished it soon thereafter.
	Bailey claimed he spoke to the Tribune at 10-10.30 to ask for an extension. Why would this be necessary in normal circumstances? With a typing speed of 20 words a minute – very slow – the typing would have taken 45 minutes. Between 8 am and noon, he had 320 minutes. The Tribune stated they had no contact from Bailey until 4-5 pm

	That was the time Bailey called in the article and dictated his story on the phone, so no fax was required.
	The Tribune said Bailey had no call until 4 to 5 pm.
	In a few brief paragraphs, Bailey's lying has been dismantled. Why did the report author fail to do so? He had all the statements.
	And had he mastered the critical thinking skills to expose the lies, he should have asked: Why is Bailey lying? Why is he giving another false alibi? Instead, he does nothing;
	No evidence of warnings by AGS
In relation to the part of the tape which apparently deals with a recording in July of 1997. Bailey asserts that there is definitely a concerted attempt to implicate him as the killer of Sophie Toscan Du Plantier. He says that he believes that the Gardaí have lied to people in France in that context and emphasises again that he is not the killer.	

He states that the Gardaí have made it very difficult for themselves in that they have told journalists continually that he is the killer.	Note how Bailey 'asserts' rather than alleges. He provides not one dot of evidence and his insinuations are not challenged by the DPP.
The recorded conversation represents the actuality of what transpired between Mangèz and Bailey. It is not incriminating but is in fact a proclamation of innocence on the part of Bailey. On tape Bailey sounds credible and convincing.	Note how Bailey 'believes' not alleges. Here too he provides no evidence to back his allegation and DPP does not challenge the what is being stated.

An astute mind would have questioned why an allegedly innocent man who claimed to be a reputable journalist would push so many fictional narratives. A more criminally aware mind might analyse so much misdirection and obfuscation. Bailey presented deceptive narratives in plain sight and the DPP could not detect them. None of this Mangèz content addresses the issue of alleged Garda warnings and their alleged impact on the communities.

The report asserts, 'On tape, Bailey sounds credible and convincing.' This is one more empty assertion. Anyone who has read the report may not be surprised to learn that the DPP thinks Bailey is credible and convincing. This was written despite the endless lies told by Bailey in his statements. There is also no evidence that Mr Sheehan had undertaken specialist training in audio analysis. He also makes a general statement about what he has heard. He is presuming to speak for everyone, or as if anyone hearing the audio would concur. It would be more accurate and honest if he had written:

'It is my personal opinion, written as someone with no expertise in audio analysis, with no reference to any other evidence to the contrary,to say that on tape Bailey sounds credible and convincing'

This would make it clear that this was only the personal opinion of a man in an office. It could then have been ignored for being irrelevant. Which is what the DPP should have done in 2001.

This section should not be in the report. It is littered with unsupported assertions, assumptions, and conclusions based only on those assumptions. There is a complete disconnect between the title of this section and its content. There is no evidence of any inappropriate conduct by the Gardai in this section.

Relationship between Gardaí and certain witnesses. (Report section 8)

This is the second AGS focussed section. It focuses primarily on two officers. One, in particular, was D/Gda. Fitzgerald. The officers worked on the Sophie Toscan du Plantier case, so it is no surprise that they had relationships with witnesses. One must assume that the DPP is implying impropriety or inappropriate conduct.

The report promptly points out that Fitzgerald identified Marie Farrell when she was supplying information anonymously. So, nothing inappropriate there. It goes on to state:

> "He is also the officer alleged to have given cash, clothes and hash to Martin Graham in order to obtain incriminating evidence against Bailey"

This is a potentially nasty insinuation. What is the point of throwing in this allegation? The report should spell out what it is trying to tell the reader. It fails to tell the readers that making payments (including the provision of items such as clothes) to informants is not in any way illegal or improper. The provision of an illegal drug would be a serious offence for a Police officer. There is no concrete evidence to support this allegation. In those circumstances the DPP should not have used the report to speculate in that way. Many years after the report a whole raft of reviews and commissions showed there to be no evidence supporting the suggestion that a citizen was given hash as payment. There was not a stitch of evidence in later years and none back in 2001.

When the report states, " obtain incriminating evidence against Bailey," it should have been noted that the phrase has a hint of ambiguity—not something that should be found in a report of this importance. The author ought to have been clear that he meant obtaining real evidence that would incriminate Bailey rather than potential false evidence that might get Bailey put in prison. Given the evidence-lite critical nature of the AGS sections, it would have been better to be clear.

The next assertion in the report does not change that. It then repeats Thomas's claim that she was 'Press Ganged' by Fitzgerald into giving 'false evidence' about Ian Bailey. This is a mere allegation; even the report author puts her claim in parenthesis. One might expect him to treat anything Thomas said with a dose of scepticism as she had made it clear she would only ever be a witness in support of Bailey. She had also provided him with a false alibi. Then he adds:

> "..while she was unlawfully in custody."

This is not a legal fact but an opinion. It is stated as if it is a fact. Not a single judge has found the arrest unlawful. There is no reason for the DPP to repeat this point of view. In the section regarding Jules Thomas, addressed in Appendix 4, the claim of unlawfulness is mentioned twice; it is mentioned one further time with reference to inconsistencies in chapter 12. This suggestion did not deserve to be raised once, let alone four times.

The report then says that Fitzgerald took a statement from a witness called Michael Oliver, a former partner of Jules Thomas and father to her two eldest daughters; that statement contradicted what Oliver had said earlier. To this, the report adds:

> "It could certainly be argued that Oliver in an attempt to avoid a heavy sentence was anxious to please the Gardaí at the time of making the statement"

All sorts of things could be argued. Maybe Oliver had found religion and made changes. Maybe he had been a friend of Bailey and tried to cover for him but had later decided to tell the truth. Maybe Oliver did nothing. There are many other things that 'could be argued'. The tried-and-tested method to determine which option is right is to check it against the facts. In this case, it was not an approach favoured by the DPP.

Nothing in the report shows Oliver received any benefits from an actual change in his story. There is no evidence that could enable anyone to arrive at a judgment about any of the options. Yet the DPP picked one. It was an option that worked in favour of Bailey and reflected poorly on AGS. This was not the only time this happened. Why was an opinion included in the report without evidence? The report asserts opinions and arguments without evidence. We still do not know why this was done.

Most of the section describes the interactions between Gards and the witness, Martin Graham, regarding payments and hash. None of this tale is indicative of illegal or improper action. Despite the abject failure to provide evidence, the report concludes that "the balance of evidence suggests that Graham is telling the truth" regarding the provision of hash. Given that the section is virtually an evidence-free zone, it is impossible to identify the evidence that the author was weighing up.

This section was rife with speculation and questionable inferences. If the aim was to suggest charges against Bailey would be unsafe because of police impropriety, then it was a miserable effort. It ought not to have been included in the report. There is nothing substantive in this section to aid a decision about Bailey. It appears as if the aim of the section was to try and find fault with individual officers.

Other aspects of Garda Investigation (Report section 13)

The thirteenth section of the DPP report is a strange item that appears almost to have been added, so a few more moans about AGS, along with a couple of dubious last-minute inferences, can be squeezed in. This is a confused mash-up of bits and pieces, and its overall contribution to the report is highly questionable. It comes in two parts. The first concerns Martin Graham and the second addresses evidence submitted by the Camiers.

Graham

The section has no introduction or explanation for what is to be found under the heading of 'other aspects.' There is a strange beginning to the section of an important legal document. It jumps straight in, saying, " Page 7 of the transcript of a tape recording made by D/Gda. Fitzgerald and D/Gda. Coughlan to discredit Martin Graham reads as follows:" This claim that the officers were setting out to discredit Graham is a very serious allegation. In keeping with the first two sections involving AGS, no evidence has been provided to support the allegation. This type of insinuation falls far below what one should expect from the DPP.

> "this could be a very important conversation Martin, there could be revelations here that could save another life and that is all we are interested in and do you know that people are scared around here, especially women that he has assaulted in the past, including his own wife you know and all we are trying to do is get the truth and save a life. When things die down, things will revert back to the old ways, drink, joints, the moon and everything you know, what is going to happen again, because there will be more reactions. Do you study the moon?"

The report then observes that Graham was poor and took drugs. It then finishes this part of the section by concluding:

> If Gardaí were prepared to discuss the case in such terms in a recorded conversation it is a fair inference that such comments were characteristic of the approach of at least some of the Gardaí. Such comments seem to have been intended to elicit a particular response from witnesses who are in effect exhorted to take a particular line in order to avoid further loss of life.

This part of the report comprises a clip from a recording, a brief biographical description of Graham, and then an inference reached by Sheehan that he declares as being 'fair.' His capacity to generalise his personal point of view is breathtaking.

First, the report states that Graham had a drug-fuelled, indigent lifestyle. One would not speak to him as one might at a Dublin dinner party. The type of things being said and how they were said would likely be appropriate given the man who was being spoken to.

A second point is the total failure to put that clip into a wider context, which was evident in the statements provided to AGS. Graham met Bailey at Russell Barrett's home immediately after his release from his first arrest on February 11th, 1996. In his statement on the 17th, Graham described his meeting with Bailey.

> 17.02.1996 From the statement by M Graham
>
> "He introduced himself and I offered him some tea, during the course of he having a cup of tea he Bailey appeared to be paranoid about the murder of the French Lady. I asked Graham if Bailey told him about the murder and his reply was yes he told me that he murdered her. I have it all up here pointing to his head. "

This demonstrated that Bailey spoke freely with Graham, and he had confessed to the murder. Graham told the investigators, 'he told me that he murdered her.' Given that it was widely known that Bailey hospitalised Thomas and he confessed to murdering Sophie, the officers were not disclosing confidential information. Telling Graham that the man who confessed to a brutal murder poses a threat to women will have come as no surprise. The DPP had Graham's statements they knew Bailey had confessed to him. Asking Graham to try and get more information is sensible. Had Graham not heard Bailey's confession it may have been a questionable request from the officers. However, Graham had heard a confession.

The whole anti-AGS premise collapses once the broader context of Bailey's confession to Graham is known. One is left wondering why the DPP failed to mention this important information. The anti-AGS conclusion now has a hollow ring to it. The insinuation in the report, 'If Gardaí were prepared to discuss the case in such terms in a recorded conversation, it is a fair inference that such comments were characteristic of the approach of at least some of the Gardaí.' now becomes ridiculous. The Gards were speaking in a way Graham himself spoke. The officers were talking about the threat that a man who confessed to Graham might pose to other women. That is eminently reasonable. Furthermore, given that Bailey had confessed to the murder of Sophie to Graham, it would also make sense to see if Bailey would disclose other information about the murder.

Then the report goes on to suggest further evidence-free opinions:

> "such comments were characteristic of the approach of at least some of the Gardaí."

Rather than the sinister imputations, one might hope all, rather than some, officers would communicate effectively with people and, when that person has heard a confession, seek to gather further information. It is hard to find any evidence supporting the conclusion that 'comments were characteristic'. Likewise, there is no indication whatsoever what 'some of the Gardaí' amounts to. Is it two people, twenty people, or two hundred people? There are no numbers and, of course, no evidence to support the assertion. There should be serious concerns that this extended 'opinion piece' consistently fails to provide evidence.

> "Such comments seem to have been intended to elicit a particular response from witnesses who are in effect exhorted to take a particular line in order to avoid further loss of life."

The report author fails to specify the 'particular responses' he implies the investigators are trying to elicit. Nor does he explain what he means by 'who are in effect exhorted to take a particular line'. What is the line he is referring to? The author balked from spelling it out. This report deserved better than vague imputations. To this day, it would be helpful if the DPP explained what was meant here. That passage also refers to witnesses, but it is no surprise that the names of all these 'influenced' witnesses are not provided. In this brief part of the report, the author segues from the two officers to 'some officers' and from Graham to 'witnesses.' Hopefully, these transitions are due to sloppy thinking and writing rather than vexatious insinuations.

In the Graham case, officers most likely sought further information about the murder Bailey had confessed to. An Garda Siochana's conduct was not corrupt, dishonest, or sinister.

Camiers

The second part of the section focuses on the evidence of James and Geraldine Camier. James spoke to Jules Thomas late in the morning on 23.12.1996. He explained how Thomas was tired and emotional when they talked to each other. Thomas told him that Bailey was in Dreenane working as a journalist on the case of a murdered French woman. In separate statements, two newspapermen said Bailey had told each of them that he had been in Dreenane at the scene of the crime at the exact same time.

The primary concern here is the statements of Geraldine Camier, who did not have a conversation with Thomas. The relevant conversation was with James. The report author is keen to take issue with James Camier's statements. In the first instant, he resorts to one of his favourite disclaimers: the statement was given almost two years after the event and is therefore suspect. The reality is that the delay in submitting a statement does not negate the content. It is something that would have been better tested in a trial than decided upon by a solicitor in a Dublin office.

The main exchange between Camier and Thomas between 11 am and 11.30 am on 23.12.1996 is described in the report. It stated that Camier was shocked by the news shared by Thomas. Then a full paragraph is dedicated to something that James Camier did not mention. He made no mention of talking to other people about the death. An officer called this both bizarre and very strange. This is of little consequence without further information, including the nature of Camier. To second guess on this subject is unnecessary, and speculating is meaningless. In a later statement, Camier said that when business became quiet, at a time that was not specified, he mentioned the murder to his wife.

On the basis of those observations, the report reached the following groundless conclusion:

> "The most charitable interpretation that one can attribute to the Camier evidence is that it is wholly unreliable."

This inference is nonsensical but helpful for Bailey. James Camier has been steadfast in his comments about his conversation with Jules Thomas on the 23rd. To reject his evidence on the grounds of who he did or did not tell about the conversation is ludicrous. All the more so because the report excluded so many statements about what happened that morning. These are spelled out in chapter three of this book. What Camier told the investigators is corroborated 100% by Cross and McSweeney, but Sheehan excludes that information. Soon after her conversation with Camier, Thomas tells her daughter about the death. This is yet another statement that supports what Camier said. Fenella Thomas stated that Thomas and Bailey went out that morning, and Fuller saw only Thomas driving to Schull, meaning Bailey was elsewhere.

For some reason, the report concluded that who James Camier did or did not speak to about the death far outweighed the core statements of Camier, Cross, McSweeney, Saffron Thomas, Fenella Thomas, and Bill Fuller. To conclude that James Camier's evidence is wholly unreliable implies that all those other people are wholly unreliable. It is nonsense. The omitted evidence is far more compelling than the DPP nitpicking. The lightweight analysis of Camier within a broader context is ridiculous. It should not be in the report without reference to all the statements supporting Camier.

The most charitable interpretation that one can attribute to this part of the DPP report is that it is wholly unreliable.

The repeated criticisms of AGS has little substance.

The dominant theme in the DPP report's first two AGS sections is the repeated absence of evidence. There was nothing tangible regarding the warnings, the content of such warnings, nor evidence that these 'invisible warnings' influenced the community. The section on the relationship between named officers and certain witnesses was, in many ways, a variation of the section on warnings. In both cases, the underlying idea appeared to be that AGS put pressure on people to make a stronger case against Bailey. If it had been true, it would have been a significant scandal. However, there was no evidence to support this theory.

In the third section, a different, three-pronged approach was used. First, a piece of information was selected from the AGS file. Second, some unfounded conclusions were drawn from the information. Third, all information that invalidated the DPP conclusions was excluded.

The DPP appeared extraordinarily keen to find fault with AGS. If faults did not exist, then they were 'suggested' or offered as the only 'reasonable' inference, even if alternatives were at least as plausible.

In some places, there is a failure to acknowledge that plenty of other sources of information raised the issue of Bailey's culpability. Just because that information was excluded does not mean it did not exist. Bailey's violence was widely known. Did the DPP believe that people in Schull did not see the black eyes and bruises of Jules Thomas? There was mention of the grapevine within rural communities but a failure to consider the implications of what that may mean. People will have heard about Bailey savagely beating Thomas in the summer of 1996. They may have spoken to one or more of the seven people in the Galley bar late on the 22[nd,] who said Bailey had no injuries when he left the bar that night. It is more than likely that the eighteen people who heard Bailey confess have told others about what he said. People such as Paul O'Colmain and Caroline Leftwick are likely to have told others how Bailey knew about the death hours before he claimed to have found out. Dozens of honest local people had first-hand evidence of Bailey's aberrant behaviour. It was not nefarious actions by Police officers that alerted the community to Bailey's potential threat. It was Bailey's conduct.

The next chapter will show how findings since 2001 have failed to support the widespread criticisms proffered in the DPP report. Two detailed in-house investigations (2002 and 2008) by An Garda Síochána led by senior officers found some failings but nothing suggesting corruption, conspiracy, or illegal conduct from the investigating officers. A lengthy civil trial (2014-15) instigated by Bailey, in which DPP officials supported him, resulted in Bailey suffering an ignominious loss and landing with a debt measured in millions of euros. Extensive investigations were conducted by the Fennelly

Commission (2017) and the Garda Síochána Ombudsman Commission (2018).

The three sections focusing on An Garda Síochána provide no evidence on which to base a decision on charging or not charging Bailey. It indicates the DPP's 'state of mind' regarding AGS. It is inconceivable that sections such as these would be included in the report if it was written today

There is no good reason why this detritus was in the report. It is unjustifiably critical of AGS and appears to imply that evidence pointing to Bailey's guilt may have been false and encouraged by AGS's actions. That is untrue. It did not happen. The DPP comments about AGS conduct had little or no basis in evidence.

CHAPTER **11**

Aftermath 2 Post-2001

Between the 2001 report and Ian Bailey's death, significant developments occurred that were relevant to the case made against An Garda Síochána and the content of the 2001 report. Nothing supported the criticisms of the police.

No corruption, no conspiracy: The role of An Garda Síochána

Few, if any, cases in Ireland have seen the police's conduct scrutinised in more detail than that of the Sophie Toscan du Plantier case. It has been reviewed twice by senior Police Officers (2002 and 2008) and has been at the heart of one of the largest civil trials in Irish legal history (2014-15). The Fennelly Commission investigated the case (2017), and there was a Gsoc report on the case (2018).

One of the ways Bailey sought to distract attention from his crime was to make frequent ridiculous claims. This applies to his repeated accusations against AGS. Useful idiots embraced his fact-free stories. Many of these people bore personal grievances regarding AGS and were happy to jump on the Bailey bandwagon. An example was the lie that AGS had lost the gate taken from Dreenane for forensic examination. This was a narrative Bailey loved. It could be used to allege AGS incompetence, corruption, and conspiracy. A few ignorant Baileyites have been keen to repeat the gate story even after Bailey's death. However, there was one difficulty with that narrative. It was a lie.

On July 13th, 2021, Senan Molony, a leading journalist on the Toscan du Plantier case, wrote an article in the Irish Independent. The headline captured the truth of the matter: 'Blood-stained gate in Sophie's murder inquiry was not 'lost', gardaí reveal '.

Molony explained what had happened to the gate. The National Forensic Laboratory, based in Dublin, decided to discard it. The NFL, not the Gardai, concluded that the gate had no evidential value for the investigation. Several bloodstains or blood smears were found on three of the five bars on the gate. All the blood was du Plantier's. Further tests were to follow, and then it was retained for six years, at which point it was disposed of. It was not lost. That was untrue.

The McNally and McAndrew reports

Following the significant proportion of the 2001 DPP report dedicated to criticising AGS, Garda Commissioner

Pat Byrne wanted a full review of the investigation; in January 2002, a review team was set up under the leadership of Chief Superintendent Austin McNally. In December of that year, the review team concluded that while no new evidence had been gathered to support the information supplied to the DPP, Ian Bailey remained a suspect.

In October 2005, Ian Bailey complained to AGS alleging Garda misconduct. The Garda Commissioner Noel Conroy appointed Assistant Commissioner Ray McAndrew to investigate the complaint. After a detailed and thorough investigation, McAndrew recommended to the DPP that there was a lack of evidence to support the complaints made by Bailey and others regarding members of the Garda Síochána. In July 2008, the DPP's James Hamilton recommended that no prosecutions be made following the McAndrew Report.

Thorough investigations based on facts and evidence exposed the lies Ian Bailey and his supporters pushed. The DPP 2001 report that 'accepted' Bailey's narrative was now proving to be deeply flawed

Bailey was determined to continue promoting his false narrative; in truth, that was how he spent the rest of his life. This led to the 2014 civil trial.

The 2014 trial

> The jury was given two questions to answer
>
> The first was: "Did gardaí Jim Fitzgerald, Kevin Kelleher, and Jim Slattery or any combination of them conspire together to implicate Mr. Bailey in the murder of Sophie Toscan du Plantier by obtaining statements from Marie Farrell by threats, inducements or intimidation which purportedly identified him as the man she saw at Kealfadda Bridge in the early hours of December 23rd, 1996 when they knew they were false?"
>
> The jury answered No.
>
> The second question was: "Did Det Garda Fitzgerald and Sergeant Maurice Walsh conspire by threats, inducements or intimidation to get statements from Marie Farrell that Ian Bailey had intimidated her, when they knew they were false?"
>
> They also answered No

In 2014 Ian Bailey attempted to sue the Garda Síochána and the Irish state for wrongful arrest for the murder of Sophie Toscan du Plantier. A trial expected to last six weeks ran for sixteen weeks. The trial heard the evidence of 93 witnesses. Bailey called 21 witnesses, while the state called 72. The Bailey case had claims of wrongful arrest, conspiracy, false imprisonment, assault, and trespass against the person. It also included the intentional inflicting of emotional harm. The defence denied every single claim and produced evidence to challenge each one.

Having heard all the evidence, Judge Hedigan explained that many of the claims should have been made within six years, and they were time-barred and, therefore, not actionable. The issue that remained for the Jury was to determine whether some gardai conspired to implicate Mr Bailey in the murder.

An important ruling from the judge was regarding Bailey's wrongful arrest. He said there were many grounds for each arrest, which did not depend on Marie Farrell's statement. The judge added that it would be "perverse" to find wrongful arrest. The issue of negligence could not be part of the case because the gardai had no duty of care in the context of investigations.

The Jury did not decide in Bailey's favour on the remaining issues, which was a humiliating defeat. Bailey's hope of being awarded millions of euros was crushed. Once again, his scurrilous and vexatious claims aimed at Garda Síochána were unwarranted. This was also the trial in which the Judge refused to let the DPP report into evidence and where the Judge had deep concerns regarding Mr. Robert Sheehan, the solicitor who wrote the report.

If the reviews and the trial outcomes were not enough to put an end to highly contentious nonsense regarding An Garda Síochána, more was to follow. Two lengthy and detailed reports from the Fennelly Commission (2017) and the Garda Síochána Ombudsman Commission (2018) should forever shut down this distraction and leave the focus on Ian Bailey.

The Fennelly Commission 2017 - Commission of Investigation (Certain Matters relative to An Garda Síochána and other persons)

> "The Commission concluded that despite "blunders" and an "underlying lack of lawful authority", the garda recording saga was not "a history of anything approaching deliberate abuse of power"

The Commission was established in 2014 and reported in 2017. Initially, it was called the Commission of Investigation (Certain Matters relative to An Garda Síochána and other persons). It was set up to investigate several controversies involving the Garda Síochána. The sole member of the commission was Nial Fennelly, a retired justice of the Supreme Court. He identified three separate strands within the commission's terms of reference. One of these was: Death of Sophie Toscan du Plantier: evidence from phone recordings at Bandon Garda station of misconduct in the investigation.

The Commission identified five telephone lines into Bandon Garda Station, where much of the investigation into Sophie Toscan du Plantier's murder was conducted. Of approximately 40,000 recorded calls, 297 were relevant to the criminal investigation. However, 166 were of no concern, while others were inaudible in parts. This left a small number of calls that did cause concern.

Tampering with evidence.

The report explained how, in a few conversations, Gardaí investigating the case had discussed the possibility of altering or suppressing evidence, but not that they had done so. Mr. Justice Fennelly found "no evidence that any of these suggestions were followed by any actual interference with or modification of evidence." While there was no evidence interference, the Commission described this behaviour as improper conduct.

The disclosure of confidential information

On a second issue, the Commission found that AGS had disclosed confidential negative information about Ian Bailey, their chief suspect, to journalists, locals, and others, including revenue officials. For example, an officer named Sgt. Alpha made seven calls over a week in which he shared information on such topics as the imminent arrest of Bailey. That he had beaten his partner to a pulp a few times, that he was drumming up a media campaign, and that some people were protecting him. While such conduct was both unacceptable and unprofessional, it was limited to a very small number of officers who, on rare occasions, conducted themselves inappropriately.

The alleged provision of drugs in order to collect incriminating evidence

Concerning officers providing an individual with drugs, it is worth noting what this thorough investigation found. The Commission's findings were clear. There was no evidence of drugs or large sums of money being given to the man. He was given some clothing and a small amount of money well within the officers' purview.

> "While the Garda members in those calls did not expressly reject such requests, there is no evidence that they agreed expressly or impliedly to supply drugs to Mr B."
>
> Paragraph 12.36
>
> "the Commission has found no evidence that any member of An Garda Síochána expressly or impliedly offered to pay substantial sums of money to"
>
> Paragraph 12.38

This reinforces the concerns about the inferences and assumptions made in the 2001 DPP report concerning the police. The Commission did not say there was insufficient or scant evidence; it said there was no evidence. Having no evidence and then jumping to some of the conclusions found in the DPP Report 2001 was a disservice to the whole process.

When all the investigations were completed and the evidence analysed, the overall conclusion was that the Garda recording saga was not "a history of anything approaching deliberate abuse of power."

GSOC report 2018 - Investigation into the complaints of Ian Bailey, Catherine "Jules" Thomas and Marie Farrell

> "There is no evidence to suggest that Ian Bailey was 'framed' for the murder or that evidence was falsified, forged or fabricated by members of the Garda Síochána."

The Commission investigated a complaint made by Ian Bailey to the Garda Síochána Ombudsman Commission (GSOC) in 2011 and complaints made by Jules Thomas and Marie Farrell in 2012. The report was published in 2018.

The report was highly critical of how the investigation was managed as evidence had gone missing. In particular, regarding the running and administration of the incident room that had been set up to investigate the murder, The report stated that "The witness statements provided to Gsoc from senior Garda members do not indicate clearly who was in charge of the investigation from the outset and through the inquiry and who was responsible for making the strategic decisions – including the arrest plans,"

While such mismanagement was concerning, the report found no evidence to support claims by Ian Bailey, Jules Thomas, and Marie Farrell that the Garda investigation into Ms Toscan du Plantier's murder in 1996 was corrupt. The report explained, "While there was evidence of a lack of administration and management of aspects of the investigation into the murder of Sophie Toscan du Plantier, there was no evidence of the high-level corruption by gardaí alleged by the complainants"

The investigators found no evidence that Farrell was coerced by gardaí into making false statements. Farrell and Bailey had alleged the coercion. The finding of no evidence strongly suggests the allegations were completely fake. Both of them lied. Secret telephone recordings made without the knowledge of gardaí showed no signs of coercion. The report stated, "The review of these phone calls indicate that Marie Farrell had been under no pressure in her interactions with a detective Garda," said Gsoc. However, it commented that the relationship between the detective and Ms. Farrell "would appear to have been questionable at times."

> "From the material reviewed by Gsoc in this investigation, it appears that there was a reasonable belief held by gardaí at that time (1997) that Ian Bailey and Jules Thomas were responsible for the murder of Sophie Toscan du Plantier. The arrests of both were therefore lawful,"

Once again, no evidence supported Bailey and Thomas's complaint that they were unlawfully arrested. This applied to both Bailey's arrests on 10.02.1997 and 27.01.1998 and, likewise, to Thomas's arrest on 22.09.2000. Concerning Thomas, this is in direct contradiction of the repeated assertion in the 2001 DPP report.

Following a full review of material collected by the Garda investigators plus the outcome of interviews with 55 witnesses, Gsoc found "no evidence sufficient to sustain either a criminal or disciplinary charge" against serving or retired officers involved.

The 2001 report's arguments regarding An Garda Síochána's conduct were threadbare and influenced by the stories told by the pathological liar Ian Bailey. Subsequent reviews, trials, and reports concluded no evidence of conspiracy, corruption, or criminal activity.

CHAPTER **12**

Inconsistencies in relation to Bailey's response to Garda questioning (Report section 6)

The title of this section provides immediate insight into the mindset of the author. The focus was to be on inconsistencies. There is no mention of Bailey's falsehoods and lies. There was no attempt to take a systematic approach to analysing the way Bailey sought to deceive the investigators. This is confirmed at the end of this lamentable assessment when the author writes

> "The fact that Bailey and Jules Thomas have made errors in their recollection does not necessarily mean they are deliberately lying. Errors made by other persons are regarded as simple mistakes in terms of recollection."
>
> DPP report page 13

This analytically woeful review reduces the profound failings of Bailey's narratives to perhaps a few inconsistencies attributable to 'errors'. The report concludes that the 'errors' are due to memory failure rather than a conscious effort to deceive the investigators. Furthermore, the quote implies that Bailey is making errors, much like other unnamed people. That was yet another statement that is not supported by any tangible evidence. Nothing is said about who these other people may be, the number of errors they made and the nature of those errors.

Here is a simple analysis that the DPP could have undertaken. It shows that Bailey's alleged inconsistencies were not a case of random forgetting, misremembering, or later remembering. There is a pattern to what Bailey did.

	Statements made and then changed.	The changes made by Bailey	Minimum Changes
1	Says he was at home, the night of the 21st. Then he gets wind of people in the Murphy household telling AGS the truth.	Bailey changes his story to being at the Murphy home. It also shows that he was lying about when he killed the turkeys and cut down the tree.	2
2	He says he left Courtyard and took a direct route home. Did not stop.	Eventually, Bailey changes his story. He knows people at the Courtyard and Galley will be questioned.	3
3	He said he was in bed from 1 am to 8 am on the 23rd. Then Thomas stops supporting his alibi	Bailey changes this story many times about what he did from 1 am to 8 am on the 23rd	20

Inconsistencies in relation to Bailey's response to Garda questioning

4	He said he was told the deceased was French. This is rigorously challenged.	Bailey changed his story in 1998 to Non-national, maybe French.	1
5	Bailey says he knew exactly where to go. This is rigorously challenged, particularly when he shifts from French to non-national, maybe French.	Bailey changes his story, He said he did not know where to go. This leads to a new story that has several iterations.	1
6	Bailey initially said he met Shirley Foster on Dreenane Lane and had a perfunctory conversation. Later, he said he did not know exactly where to go to find the crime scene and no longer had an explanation for why he met Foster halfway down the lane.	Bailey changes the place where he says he met Foster from halfway along Dreenane Lane to the junction of Dreenane Lane and the Dunmanus-Toormore Road.	1
7	Following on from point 5, Bailey shifts from knowing exactly where to go to needing to find out in some other way.	Bailey changes his story about his conversation with Foster. She tells him where to find the crime scene in the new version.	1

8	Bailey was no longer going directly to Dreenane and was challenged as to why he was driving down the Dunmanus— Toormore Road.	Bailey changes his story to say he was going down that road to go to the Post Office, not Dreenane [this came after 2001]	1
9	Bailey was challenged as to why he would drive the long way around to the Post Office, which would double the travel time.	Bailey never got around to adapting his story yet again. He did not answer [this came after 2001]	?
10	Bailey said he went to the post office to get the name of the French cottage owner. This would mean he knew who the victim was when having no reason to know that was so.	Bailey changes his story to going to the Post office for no particular reason & was not to get the name of the cottage owner. Someone there proffers a name. Bailey embellishes and refines it	2+

All these substantial changes are not random. The overwhelming majority of them came before 2001. They cannot be attributed to 'inconsistencies' or 'memory errors'. They are consistent in terms of Bailey's approach to providing information. First, he gives false information, then he is caught giving false information or pressured to explain what he said and eventually responds by giving different false information. The table demonstrates that there was a method in Bailey's dishonesty, and his dishonesty should have been tested in court.

If this inability to analyse the evidence were not enough of a reason to dismiss this part of the report, and it is more than enough, there are also the inclusions of apparently random thoughts by the author that the DPP saw fit to keep in the report.

The report got the subject of inconsistencies and lies dreadfully wrong, and this contributed to over twenty-five years of needless suffering for Sophie's family.

Random inclusions

The report section sought to explore what Bailey said to the investigators and determine whether he was inconsistent. Despite that objective, several strange information items and one appalling factual error creep into the report.

For an unknown reason, the report included one of Ian Bailey's many ficticious theories of alternative murderers. How did this digression help the DPP evaluate Bailey's level of consistency? The only way it could would be to show how Bailey would say anything to distract those people investigating the case.

> **Carbonnet**
>
> "Bailey's response was that he believed from his investigative research that there was definitely a French connection.
>
> This Office and the Gardaí are aware that Bruno Carbonnet, a French man who was a lover of Sophie during the course of her marriage to Daniel Toscan Du Plantier stayed on occasion in her West Cork home."

The report comments regarding Carbonnet appear deeply disingenuous. Eamon Barnes, a senior figure in the DPP, had written to the French in early January 1997 requesting information about Carbonnet. The Frenchman was questioned extensively. He produced a card receipt showing he was in France on the 23rd. Carbonnet was ruled out easily and quickly. Given those facts, why did the report fail to share that information? This is a very peculiar and regrettable inclusion in the report.

If the inclusion of an alternative suspect was not bizarre enough, the decision to include the next point in this section defies credulity. Sheehan thinks his observation, without any context or alternative options, is worth raising. It is difficult to understand why the report's author thought the route from Dreenane to the Prairie cottage in the early hours of the 23rd had a bearing on Bailey's level of inconsistency.

> **Interestingly?**
>
> Interestingly, in the context of Bailey's home, Kealfadda is not on the way to or from Sophie's residence.

It is almost as if this point was an afterthought that was 'jammed into' this section.

The section is also encumbered with two of the DPP's favourite idées fixes in the brief report. It finds time to roll out the assertion that the arrest of Thomas was unlawful; it was not. It was done with reference to the phrase 'fruit of the poison tree'. A popular phrase in USA television programmes like Law and Order in the Noughties. The second idée fixe is the fixation on a particular 'theory of memory.' In this case, it is called upon to excuse Bailey's inaccuracies. However, the report does not provide any evidence to show the falsehoods are based on a real cognitive impairment. It is an excuse, not an explanation.

> **Poison trees**
>
> "It should also be noted that anything said by Bailey during the course of his detention may be inadmissible on the basis that much of what was put to him was gleaned from Jules Thomas during the course of her unlawful detention and the fruit of the poison tree rule might well apply."

> **The DPP theory of memory**
>
> "Bailey's first questionnaire was completed eight days later. It is a difficult exercise for any person to recall with precision the timing and location of ordinary matters even after a very short time."

A final inclusion is an unconscionable error. It demonstrates a sloppy approach that belies the seriousness of the report. The report states that the Studio is directly beside the house. The truth is these two buildings are 200 metres apart, the approximate length of two football or rugby pitches. The buildings are not a few second's walk apart; rather, they are three minutes apart. How on earth does the report author, every fact checker, and reader within the DPP fail to grasp that fact? Imagine being a member of Sophie's family or friends and seeing this failure in detail.

> **200 metres is not beside**
>
> "Bailey does not state that he left the home premises. He states that he went to his studio, which is located on the Thomas lands. It is directly beside the house."

These examples illustrate a lack of precision. A lack of appropriate analytical skills will also be shown when the rest of the section is addressed.

Inconsistencies?

The choice of the word inconsistency immediately shows the way the author of the report perceives the conduct of Ian Bailey. There are no references to falsehoods, untruths, or lies. To be consistent, Bailey would be expected to behave and answer questions the same way every time a similar situation occurs. Two issues ought to be researched in this context. First, was Ian Bailey consistent or inconsistent? If there are inconsistencies, there should be a clear description of what they were and their relevance to whether Bailey should be charged. Second, if there are inconsistencies, what underpins them? It is not enough to say there were inconsistencies and no more. If a suspect in a murder case is inconsistent, it is imperative to find out why he or she is behaving that way. Regrettably, there was no such rigour in this report.

Was Ian Bailey consistent or inconsistent?

The DPP report effectively concludes that Bailey was not inconsistent. Towards the end of the section, the report says Bailey and Thomas made 'errors'. There is no attempt to quantify the number of 'errors' nor point out where they occurred. There is an assertion by the report author that errors made by others have been regarded as mistakes of recollection. The implication is that someone, presumably investigating officers, had been biased in their work and conclusions. Another case of AGS 'bad' Bailey 'good'.

> "The fact that Bailey and Jules Thomas have made errors in their recollection does not necessarily mean they are deliberately lying. Errors made by other persons are regarded as simple mistakes in terms of recollection."

The first problem with the DPP work on this section is the near-total lack of details. There is nothing to say how many errors were made by Bailey nor by the nondescript 'other persons'. Nor is there any indication on the topics where 'errors' were said to have happened. This made it impossible to look for patterns. It was lamentable. There was no clarity on what Mr. Sheehan meant by a mistake, an error, or a lie. This vagueness is unhelpful, and it does justice a disservice. In chapter two, 24 factual changes by Bailey were highlighted. In chapter 4, we saw how Bailey was insistent that Cassidy said the victim was French and then was equally insistent that the victim was a non-national, possibly French. One time, Bailey said he knew exactly where to go, and then he said he found the crime scene because of a chance meeting with Shirley Foster at a junction. He went from meeting Foster on a lane that goes only to Dreenane to meet her at a junction. His explanation of going to the post office to get the French cottage owner's name turns into a story of going to the post office for no reason and learning about the victim by a further chance. There were different versions of events on when he chopped down a tree and killed 3 turkeys, who he did it with, and the injuries he incurred. In the case of Ian Bailey, it is hard to find things about which he has been consistent.

For the remainder of this chapter, the provision of untrue statements will be called falsehoods. A person who repeatedly tells investigators falsehoods should be deemed untrustworthy. If a person makes false statements with the deliberate intent to deceive and mislead, then he or she is a liar

Falsehoods

In part one of this book, Bailey's falsehoods are in abundance. For example, to say you were at home all night when you were sleeping at someone else's home is a falsehood not an error. Particularly as he only came clean when he knew he would be found out. Unless Bailey had some delusional impairment, the most likely inference is that Bailey deliberately provided false information. This pattern is seen in so many of the changes identified in part one of this book and summarised in the table earlier in this chapter.

The repeated changes in his narrative were deliberate rather than attributable to misremembering errors. Creating new versions is an attempt to obfuscate the truth rather than to reveal it. Presenting falsehoods is done to deceive. Bailey was lying. This was not a case of merely being inconsistent. Alarmingly the DPP never once suggested that Bailey lied. It beggars belief. If DPP staff could not identify all the 'inconsistencies' in Bailey's statements, then they could not address the underlying pathological dishonesty. Bailey was given a free pass.

Bailey's repeated desire to embellish his narrative, add new elements to address challenges to it, and completely change his story when the original narrative has been disassembled all point to a man who is dishonestly seeking to hide the truth.

In his 31.12.1996 statement, he goes into considerable detail in his attempt to explain why he drove directly to the remote Dreenane area. Almost twenty years after the murder, Bailey had been claiming he did not know where to go. He came up with a tale that he was going to the post office for some unexplained purpose. When his False Alibi fell apart, he came up with several new scenarios that bore no resemblance to his being asleep in bed all night. The changes made by Bailey, if one took the care to identify them, were contrived. They were false. They were intentional. They were lies.

All the circumstantial evidence demonstrating Bailey's guilt was neither identified nor understood, and the reasons for this remain unknown. Instead of musings about Carbonnet, poison trees, or strange theories of memory, the report should have uncovered Ian Bailey's persistent falsehoods.

When all the evidence is included, there can be no other conclusion than Bailey was repeatedly and systematically giving false evidence. Forget inconsistencies in his response; he lied The report got it wrong, grievously so.

The false alibi that never was

In a section on inconsistencies, it is remarkable that the author failed to highlight a false alibi. Bailey insisted that he was in bed between 1 am and 8 am on 23.12.1996. Initially, Jules Thomas confirmed his story. While Sheehan described the event, he steadfastly refused to call it what it was: a false alibi. If there is an unwillingness to name this most blatant and damning lie, there could be little hope that this section would be anything other than a Bailey whitewash.

Tribune – Not all the news that's fit to print

The DPP report refers to Bailey's claim he was given an extension to the 24th for his Tribune article. In chapter three, it was explained that this narrative was Bailey's account. The report excluded the statements of two senior Tribune journalists who gave an alternative and far more believable summary of events. That Bailey did not call them nor get an extension on the 23rd. They stated that they tried to contact Bailey that morning when chasing up his article, but no one answered the phone. In his tale about the delayed article, Bailey failed to specify who he allegedly spoke to or the new deadline. He also forgot to say he phoned in the article around 4 p.m. on the 23rd.

There is a stark choice between what Bailey says and the journalists. Their statements are incompatible. The Bailey version, told by a liar, only came into existence when his false alibi collapsed. The alternative comes from two reputable journalists explaining how they dealt with a freelancer who could not hit his deadline. The DPP report fails to address the evidence from the Tribune journalists while regurgitating Bailey's uncorroborated tale.

There is the possibility that Bailey had all but finished his article before the Christmas weekend. In doing so, he was free to spend the weekend doing very little work and drinking heavily in the evenings. This would explain why he initially did not mention working on his article, because he did not do so. The continually changing story of the article only came into existence when he learned that Thomas was not supporting his false alibi.

The inference to be drawn here is that Bailey lied to the investigators about where he was between 1 a.m. and 1.40 p.m. on 23.12.1996. When he was found out, he devised his 'Tribune story'. The new story was full of holes. His statements about what he was doing with his time that weekend suggest his article was completed. The statements from the Tribune journalists show Bailey's new version was a pack of lies.

The man who rebutted himself

The report writes of Bailey, "His version of events cannot be properly rebutted." This is nonsense, as anyone who has taken the time to read the statements will know. A rebuttal is a form of evidence that is presented to contradict or nullify other evidence. In most cases, this is done as part of an adversarial process. In this case, it is Bailey who rebuts himself time and time again. He says he was in bed all night and then says he got up for several hours, thereby presenting evidence that contradicts his earlier evidence; he says he was told the deceased was French and then says he was told she was a non-national, possibly French. Once again, the new evidence nullifies the earlier version. In his statements, Bailey rebuts himself and exposes his lies over two dozen times. The staff at the DPP appears to have been blind to all of them. Blind to more than two dozen changes of fact. This might be funny if it was not so tragic. Did no one at the DPP conduct a rigorous analysis? To see the endless contradictions requires one to see the inconsistencies in Bailey's evidence. The DPP saw none of it. To the DPP, Bailey was not inconsistent and did not contradict himself. They got it wrong.

Enough!

In the DPP report, Sheehan writes about Bailey's description of what he did on the morning of the 23rd. It is found in the box below. It is an accurate, verbatim presentation of what Bailey said. However, the DPP fails to provide a broader context. They chose Bailey's version given on the evening of 10.02.97. The report fails to mention five other versions Bailey gave between 1996 and 1998. Analysing inconsistencies is impossible when five of six versions are excluded. If there were inconsistencies, then there may be falsehoods and lies. Surely in a document of such importance, an officer of the DPP would be rigorous.

> "Bailey stating "some time after going to bed I got up – did a bit of writing in the kitchen. I then went down to the studio. I am not sure what time it was but it was dark. I have no watch. I had a story to write for the Tribune and was told it was O.K. – that Tuesday would do. It was a story about the Internet. I went back to Jules's house about 11:00 a.m."

First, let us look at Bailey's first couple of statements about what he was doing in the early hours of 23.12.1996. His first statement came on December 31st, 1996, and the second one was given the morning he was arrested on 10.02.1997.

31.12.1996	10.02.1997 9.40 am
Awake at 8a.m. - 9a.m. on Monday 23.12.1996, got up and made coffee. Jules in bed. Returned to bed with coffee. Tuned into Gaelic. Got up again at 10a.m. Was going to go to Skibbereen in the early afternoon, but Cassidy's phone call changed that so I was just "pottering" around until that.	Got up early, made coffee for Jules and brought it to bed. It was about 9.30a.m.-10a.m. went back to bed listened to the Radio. Spoke about what had to be done and we were going to Skibbereen, Co. Cork together, to deliver a turkey and do some shopping.

There is a significant shift in the time Bailey got up to make coffee. Other than that, the statements are consistent with each other. In both cases, little activity was reported for the rest of the morning, leading up to the call from

Inconsistencies in relation to Bailey's response to Garda questioning   215

Eddie Cassidy. In both cases, Bailey said he went to bed with Jules from approximately 1 am to 1,30 am, awoke later, and made coffee. In his 10.02.97 statement made at 5.30 pm, Bailey emphasises that he slept through the night beside Thomas. However, another statement was made on the 10th of February on the very same subject just a few hours later.

10.02.1997 9.40 am	Signed 10.02.1997 Early evening
Got up early, made coffee for Jules and brought it to bed. It was about 9.30a.m.-10a.m. went back to bed listened to the Radio. Spoke about what had to be done and we were going to Skibbereen, Co. Cork together, to deliver a turkey and do some shopping.	Some time after going to bed I got up - Did a bit of writing - the kitchen. I then went down to the studio I am not sure what time it was but it was dark. I have no watch. I had a story to write for Tribune and was told it was okay that Tuesday would do. It was a story about the Internet. I went back to Jules house at about 11a.m.
5,30 Q. Did you leave the house after going home with Jules? A.I went to bed, I stayed in bed all night until next morning, I never left the house that night, Jules will tell ye.	

The DPP report singled out the 10.02.97 early evening statement. A casual reader may have assumed that was Bailey's only statement on the subject or that the statement was typical of all the others. This was not the case. The 1996 and the first statement in 1997 were very similar. They bear no resemblance to the version selected by the DPP. In the early statements, Bailey sleeps all night, does the coffee-making and back-to-bed routine, and finally potters about. The statement selected by Sheehan is one where he wakes up, works in the kitchen, walked 200 metres in the dark to the studio – for no apparent reason – and stays there until 11 am. The whole making coffee, going back to bed, listening to the radio, and planning the day ahead with Thomas has been jettisoned.

The DPP leaves out the first two statements, which include Bailey's false alibi. We have already seen how the report does not explicitly reference a false alibi. In this section, the false alibi is excluded. This is not good enough. How can anyone claim to be analysing inconsistencies yet exclude them from the report?

When the statement selected for the report is put into context one is forced to ask 1. What was going on regarding Bailey? 2. How could the DPP fail to see the significant changes made by Bailey on the same day? Soon, we will return to these questions. Before that, there are some further statements made by Bailey that must be highlighted.

Inconsistencies in relation to Bailey's response to Garda questioning   217

11.02.1997 0.05 am	27.01.1998 12.25 pm	27.01.1998 8.02 pm
Now you have told the other officer that you in fact did get up that night and left Jules house. **Yes I now remember that I did get up and go to my studio.** (Rented house) to do some work. Why are you now changing your story regarding that night, is it because you are aware that Jules is now saying that you did get up. No, "**I remember now**".	Q. Tell us exactly what is the position in relation to the night of the 22nd/23rd December, 1996 when you arrived home with Jules? A. We just went to bed. Q. Did you stay in bed? A Well no I got out of bed o.k. Q. Where did you go? A. I went into the kitchen and did some writing. Q. Did you leave the house? A. I did go to my studio in the morning by this I mean 9 a.m roughly, I had an article to write for the Tribune.	Lied to police in his original questionnaire and statement. **I did not lie to you - we didn't have the right story.** He stated "I went to bed about 1.30a.m. - 2 a.m. Up at 4 a.m. to write -30/35 minutes writing - then back to bed. Got up at 9 a.m. and went down to Studio to finish the article.

Following the volte-face from the morning narrative in 1997 to the afternoon narrative, one further statement was made during Bailey's first arrest. In this one, he became keen to make an excuse for the dramatic changes. He said, " Yes, I now remember that I did get up and go to my studio," and "I remember now". Even Bailey knows the changes are dramatic and require some explanation. This is something that the report missed. A diligent reviewer of the evidence would instinctively want to find the cause of this prise de conscience. It would appear that the DPP decided these were inconsequential errors rather than significant changes in the narrative.

Bailey had not finished with his ever-changing narratives. However, you would not know it from the DPP report. In his 1998 interrogation, he produces two further versions. The man who said he did not have a watch in the preferred DPP option suddenly can give precise timings. In the DPP option, Bailey writes in the kitchen and immediately goes to the Studio until 11 am. In his final version, Bailey gets up, writes from 4 am to 4.35 am, and then returns to bed for four and a half hours. Only then, at 9 am, does he go to the Studio. By this point, Bailey had long left mere inconsistencies behind him. He is refuting his own statements and repeatedly offering one falsehood after another. Yet the DPP saw none of it. Furthermore, the report's readers saw none of these other Bailey versions because Sheehan chose not to include them in his final report.

In further comments, Bailey said, "I did not lie to you - we didn't have the right story." Even the slowest brain would see that Bailey is conceding that he had offered a 'wrong story'. He is also suggesting that the 'wrong' story came from him and one or more other people. Even comments like these were ignored by the DPP.

The box below shows us Bailey's early position and his final description in his 1998 statement. If the DPP honestly believed this was not a paradigm shift in Bailey's narrative, then the report was damned from its inception.

| In bed all night [The false alibi] | He stated "I went to bed about 1.30a.m. - 2 a.m. Up at 4 a.m. to write -30/35 minutes writing - then back to bed. Got up at 9 a.m. and went down to Studio to finish the article. |

A brief thought experiment

Imagine that all Bailey's versions above were put together on a single page. Do you think any sensible, intelligent person could read them and conclude that there were no inconsistencies, falsehoods, or lies?

"Coup de Grâce"

Returning to the dramatic switch in Bailey's narrative on 10.02.1997, it defies credulity that DPP staff could read the morning and afternoon statements and not be shocked by the changes; if the Bailey statement concerning the morning of the 23rd selected by the DPP were true, then the statements in 1996 – 1997 were consistently false. Repeating so many falsehoods is no 'error'; it is a systematic attempt to deceive. The report author should have homed in on it rather than giving it a free pass.

This brings us to the issue of what could lead to such a dramatic change. Immediately before Bailey dramatically changes his story, there was the following exchange.

> "It was then put to him that Jules stated that he left the bed and returned the following morning with a mark on his forehead.
>
> He denied this."

The investigators had told Bailey that Thomas had blown his false alibi. She would no longer vouch for Bailey being with her all night. If Bailey had been a truthful man and given an honest account, he could have stuck with what he said in 1996. But he had been caught in his lies, so he had to concoct another fictitious narrative on the spot.

This left Bailey needing to create a narrative that could explain his absence from bed for several hours. Like any seasoned liar, he produced something. He sought to impress his 'listener' by adding embellishments and elaboration, not realising that people could see through his pattern of behaviour. His narcissism resulted in him thinking he could pull the wool over anyone's eyes. He believed himself clever and most other people stupid. This delusion contributed to his undoing.

The information is there. The dramatic changes in the statements were triggered by Bailey being caught out on his false alibi. These were not mere errors or 'inconsistencies. They were falsehoods told to deceive. They were lies. Sadly, for some reason, the DPP decided otherwise.

When most people find themselves stuck in a deep hole, they stop digging. Mr Sheehan added a further comment.

> "We know that Bailey wanted to pursue his career as a journalist and this could explain why he got up in order to write the story."

There is nothing wrong with someone wanting to pursue a career. Bailey getting up early or late is not the point. The point is that Bailey gave a false alibi. When the false alibi collapsed, a whole new story popped up. If this new career was so important, why had he forgotten about it in 1996 and early 1997? Why would the exposure of his false alibi lead to a spontaneous recalling of his writing activities that morning?

If the DPP hypothesis is taken to its logical conclusion, it means that, for some bizarre reason, Bailey and Thomas gave AGS a false alibi to hide the fact that Bailey was writing an article about the internet for the Tribune. What a circus.

It is difficult to imagine how the DPP described Bailey's ever-changing stories as typical errors no different from anyone else. The minimisation of what Bailey did is scandalous. It is impossible to understand how DPP staff read Bailey's statements and concluded there was no systematic deceit.

His story cannot and should not be believed. On this one issue there was enough evidence to charge Ian Bailey and test his evidence in a trial. The failure of the 2001 report to call Bailey to account for his lies and deceptiveness should render it obsolete.

Statements that were excluded from this section of the 2001 report
Appendix 2: pt 1 pt 2 pt 3 pt 5 pt 6 pt 7

CHAPTER **13**

Scratches, Confessions, and Did Bailey Know Sophie

The three 2001 DPP report sections addressed in this chapter focus on the same material as chapters 7, 8 and 9 in this book. The sections evaluate the evidence of Bailey's scratches, his confessions, and whether or not he knew Sophie. One might reasonably expect an analysis of the evidence to lead to similar conclusions. This is not the case. The conclusions of the DPP and this book could not be farther apart. The reasons for this can be attributed to two key differences between the analyses. These are:

1. The DPP included many 'pro-Bailey' assumptions which are not underpinned by evidence. This book does not,
2. The DPP excluded more than 60 statements that pointed towards Bailey murdering Sophie. This book includes them.

Scratches (Report section 10)

Chapter seven of this book discusses scratches. There are stark differences between that chapter and the DPP report. The two most important issues are the DPP evaluation of the statements from Bailey and Thomas and the exclusion of key statements made by people at the Galley bar on the night of 22.12.1996.

The report examined the statements from Ian Bailey, Jules Thomas, Saffron Thomas, and Virginia Thomas and concluded that Bailey's statements were supported by Jules Thomas and her two eldest daughters.

> "Bailey has consistently stated that he received scratches by climbing up a twenty-foot tree with a bow saw in one hand, cutting the top off the tree and pulling it down through the branches. Bailey is supported in his explanation as to how he got the scratches by Jules Thomas and her daughters Virginia and Saffron. "

The first sentence is factually incorrect. It states, " Bailey has consistently stated that he received scratches. " Bailey was not consistent. He first said he was cut with the bow saw, and the cuts healed. On another occasion, he said he was slightly marked by a turkey and got more scratches later. He also said that he got the scratches while dragging the Christmas tree through the branches of the rest of the tree. There should be no pretence that 'cuts from a bow saw' are the same as scratches from tree branches. After his first explanation of injuries from a bow saw, he never again mentioned getting cut that way. If that were not inconsistent enough, he gave two different causes of his cut to the head. One cause was a turkey that was being killed. The other was some accident with his staff

In chapter seven, it is clear that The Prairie occupants' statements are riddled with contradictions and inconsistencies. The DPP report stated, "Bailey is supported in his explanation as to how he got the scratches by Jules Thomas and her daughters Virginia and Saffron." Unsurprisingly, the report author does not tell us which of Bailey's two incompatible explanations the others supported. Jules Thomas was not present at the cutting down of the tree, and it remains unclear whether one or both of the daughters were present. The women offer widely different and incompatible descriptions of Bailey's injuries. Despite Bailey walking around in shorts and rolled-up sleeves, the Thomas women had wide variations on his alleged injuries.

Jules Thomas said he had scratches on his forearms. Saffron said he had scratches on his hands, arms, and legs, and Virginia only mentioned the injury to his hands. When Bailey spoke of scratches, he could not specify where they were. This is not corroborative evidence. There are no grounds to believe any of the witnesses. It is impossible to fathom how someone can read the statements of the three Thomas women and conclude they consistently support any of Bailey's scratches stories,

A breathtaking decision

In addition to reaching unfounded conclusions in support of the Bailey narrative, Sheehan made a breathtaking decision. He would leave out all the statements that indicate that Bailey got his scratches after leaving the Galley bar around 12 am on the 23rd of December. Earlier, the statements of seven people in the Galley are described in detail. Every one of these people was standing or sitting close to Bailey. None of them saw any injuries. At the very least, the report should have explained why all these people got it completely wrong in the opinion of the DPP.

The only reference to the seven witnesses comes when the report says, "From the evidence available, it seems clear that the scratches caused to Bailey by cutting the tree and killing the turkeys were not of a very grave nature and it is not therefore surprising that certain patrons in a pub on the night of 22 December 1996 did not observe them." Somehow seven people giving fully corroborative statements become 'certain patrons'. The statements are convincing, yet he excluded them all. The report did not even inform the readers that seven people said they saw no injuries. There is no difficulty for the DPP to accept Saffron saying there were scratches on Bailey's arms, hands, and legs or Bailey saying he was cut with a saw, but come the evening, all these injuries became invisible.

The report author mentions only one man named Tisdall in the Galley. This is because he said he may have seen slight scratches on one of Bailey's hands. This appears to lend tenuous support to the statements of the Prairie witnesses. It does not do so unless one is willing to believe that after the alleged injuries witnessed by the Prairie people, the saw cuts mentioned by Bailey, and the scratches to legs, forearms, and on one of Bailey's hands disappeared by the time Tisdall saw Bailey. The scratches seen by Tisdall were far less severe than those seen by witnesses from the 23rd onwards. This must mean something caused the heavier scratching after Bailey left the bar.

This part of the report is a nonsense. First, the Prairie witnesses provide a shambolic inconsistent series of statements. Their statements could only be believed if one were to accept that Bailey's injuries happened in the afternoon, disappeared for the evening, and then returned worse than before some time on the 23rd. The most plausible narrative for the facts is that Bailey received very limited and slight injuries or no injuries in the afternoon. In a well lit bar, seven people saw no injuries at all and one slight scratch on one hand. After leaving the Galley, Bailey sustained more substantial scratch injuries plus a cut to the head.

When all the evidence is included, and the Prairie evidence is analysed correctly, the reasonable inference is that sometime after leaving the bar, Ian Bailey received noticeable scratches to his hands and arms, plus a cut to his head. The weight lent to the chaotic Prairie statement is without merit, and the omission of the seven Galley statements is indefensible.

Bailey received the injuries after midnight on December 22nd.

For statements, see Appendix 2: pt 8

Alleged informal admissions by Bailey (Report section 9)

A recurring theme throughout the DPP report is the widescale omission of statements that point to Bailey's guilt. The section on confessions is no different. There are at least 12 known confessions that eighteen people witnessed. These are described in chapter 8. The approach of the DPP on this matter is similar to the approach taken to the analysis of scratches. Large swathes of evidence in statements are excluded. Regarding the confessions included in the report there is reason for disbelieving the analysis. The confessions are not rejected on the grounds of evidence but on the grounds of assumptions put forward by the DPP.

The confession statements included by the DPP and dismissed

The report included five of the twelve confessions based on the statements of six people. (Ungerer, Callanan, Reed, McKenna, and the Shelleys).

Yvonne Ungerer

> "He said that he had got up out of bed to do some work on an article and he went out. That must have been the time they saw me. around 4.00a.m."

> Statement by Ungerer regarding Bailey's reply when she asked him about being seen in the area of Kealfadda bridge at 4 am on 23.12.1996

In dismissing the Ungerer statement, Sheehan makes the following points. First, he asserts that it was clear that Bailey was not confessing but telling her what the Gardai were saying to him. The reader will wait in vain for evidence to support this DPP inference. There is none. This is his assumption stated as fact. We do know that two people, Ungerer and Bailey, had a conversation.

> **Yvonne Ungerer statement 11.02.1997**
>
> She asked Bailey:
>
> "Why did they arrest you? And he replied that some witnesses had come forward who had seen him down by the water or causeway. I asked him what time was that and he said that it was early in the morning. I think he said as I have already told you in a previous statement that Ian told me that he was going home that night at about 1.30a.m. with Jules but this morning he admitted to me that there was some time unaccounted for. He said that he had got up out of bed to do some work on an article and he went out. That must have been the time they saw me. around 4.00a.m."
>
> "I said what were you doing there (the causeway)and he said "Oh, I suppose I was washing the blood off my clothes", I felt he said that in a half joking way."

Robert Sheehan was not present and had no recording of the conversation. He did not hear what Bailey said or how it was said. He had no reason to assume that Ungerer was cognitively incapable of knowing what was said to her. He should have known when writing the report that Bailey was a pathological liar. He would also have known that Bailey had confessed to other people on the same day. From various statements, there were clear indications that Bailey was perturbed. The evidence of perturbation and the other confession on the same day were excluded. This misled readers of the report.

Sheehan wrote, "It is clear that Bailey was simply reciting what the Gardaí alleged to him while he was in custody." It is impossible to find anything in Ungerer's statement that suggests Bailey was reciting what someone said. There is never any reported reference to Bailey telling Ungerer that someone claimed or alleged such a thing happened. Ungerer tells the investigators, "He said that he had gotten out of bed to do some work on an article, and he went out. That must have been the time they saw me. (aro)und 4.00a.m" It was only the previous afternoon that Bailey had changed his story from sleeping all night to going out to the studio. He does not tell Ungerer that he went to the studio, not the causeway. He is not reciting what he was told. He appears to conflate what AGS raised with his 'current' story and the potential true story. This is speculation on my part. But far less speculative than the DPP stating opinions like they were facts.

In her statement, Ungerer quotes Bailey saying, "Oh, I suppose I was washing the blood off my clothes". Sheehan says this "answer is not an admission it is a sarcastic retort". He is implying that Ungerer did not pick up on the sarcasm. This is untrue, as in her statement, Ungerer says that she believed Bailey was 'half joking' when he said washing blood. Her statement suggests that she was attuned to half-joking or sarcasm and judged him to be giving a true confession.

For the report to conclude that Ungerer failed to comprehend that Bailey was allegedly being sarcastic is offensive and based upon an opinion that came four years after the event. Not a scintilla of evidence was produced to suggest Ungerer could not identify sarcastic comments or be prone to 'mishear' things.

Helen Callanan

> "I said to her as a joke that I was the murderer and that I did it to further my career".
>
> Bailey quoted in the 2001 report

Helen Callanan was a highly skilled journalist, yet the DPP thought it could better evaluate what Bailey said even though the confession happened years before and many kilometres away from Dublin. She reported the confession in one of her statements. As with Ungerer, Sheehan decided that Bailey's confession was an act of sarcasm, and Callanan was so lacking in social skills and reading nonverbal signals that she took Bailey's untrue sarcasm to be the truth.

It is important that we remind ourselves that Sheehan was not present for this discussion and had no recordings of it.

Despite this, he is confident enough to write, " his remarks to her reek of sarcasm not veracity." This is an amazing conclusion for someone not present. The key to detecting sarcastic comments is to hear the words and note the tone and inflections used by the speaker. The clear implication was the DPP knew better than Callanan. Somehow, the DPP was aware of the intonations and inflections four years later. While the woman having the conversation in real-time was missing the point. It is arrogant to imply that these two women could not comprehend what Bailey was communicating. The DPP appeared to struggle with the idea that the women were better placed to say what they heard. It is also difficult to understand why the DPP so readily believed the inveterate liar over honest witnesses.

One further comment made by the DPP was," It is quite clear that Bailey wanted to find out who was slandering him." What could this mean? The DPP does not state ' allegedly slandering him' or 'people he claimed were slandering him'. It is almost as if people at the DPP thought Bailey was being slandered. There should have been greater clarity on this point. No one at the DPP was part of the conversation. There are no solid grounds for inferring that Bailey was being sarcastic. They should not suggest Bailey was being slandered. This evidence-free assumption should not have appeared in the 2001 report.

Malachi Reed

> "I went up there with a rock one night and bashed her fucking brains in".
>
> [He then said he did it to get a story for the newspapers.]
>
> Statement by Malachi Reed regarding what Bailey said to him.

In his approach to the Reed confession, Sheehan shifts from one where he thinks he can detect sarcasm across time and distance better than two intelligent, educated women to one where he can 'read' a person's thoughts and feelings years after the event, In the case of Malachi Reed, this new skillset was 'apparently' being applied. Reed was a teenage boy who lived in the same area as Bailey. It was customary for neighbours to give each other a lift to or from Schull. Reed's mother had done so, many times for the Thomas daughters.

On February 4th, 1997, almost a week before Bailey was arrested for the first time, he was giving Reed a lift home. There were indications that Bailey had been drinking. During the journey, the subject of the murder not surprisingly came up. In a shocking outburst, Bailey said, "I went up there with a rock one night and bashed her fucking brains in." He added that he did it to get a story for the newspapers. Reed and his mother reported the events to the investigators a few days later. Reed's mother had stated that she was unaware that her son had witnessed the outburst until Malachi was openly upset on the 5th. This led Sheehan to conclude that the events had not upset Malachi at the time it happened on the 4th.

There is no evidence that someone at the DPP had some psychic gift that enabled them to read the minds and feelings of people across time and space. The truth is no one can make such a claim. Not content with one act of clairvoyance, a second one soon follows. The report says, "following his conversation with Gda. Kelleher he became upset and turned a conversation which had not apparently up until then alarmed him into something". In some way, the DPP divined what happened between the officer and the teenager all those years ago. This is intolerable stuff. The assumption that the boy and his mother were manipulated, that the officer behaved inappropriately, and that Bailey was the innocent party is consistent with the general tone of the report.

For Sheehan, it appeared it was inconceivable that a teenager might become introspective after hearing a drunken man make such appalling comments. He does not have an iota of evidence to support his 'mind reading' narrative. He offers no logical reason why a fourteen-year-old would lie in this way. These are not inferences drawn by a logical analysis of the facts. They are assumptions and speculations born of nothing concrete. The rejection of the Reed evidence is based purely on assumptions made by the

DPP. The assumptions are weak and do not justify rejecting the young man's evidence.

J McKenna

> "McKenna states that Bailey said to him do you know about the murder in the town and he said that he had seen it on T.V. in the North, Bailey turned around and said "that is me". He smirked at me as he said it."

On April 8, 1997, James McKenna, a cab driver on holiday in Schull, spoke to Ian Bailey and Jules Thomas in a bar. During their conversation, McKenna said that Ian Bailey confessed to being the murderer. Robert Sheehan seeks to discredit McKenna's evidence in several ways. First, he claims that McKenna was 'swayed' by the response of people in the bar after Bailey and Thomas left.

> "Bailey and Jules Thomas left the premises and the bar girl came running around to say, "do you know who you were with? he is the person who killed the girl. All the bar clapped".
>
> "Again this demonstrates hysteria and resentment against Bailey."

It is remarkable to witness the wide range of psychological characteristics being attributed to people in West Cork on the flimsiest evidence. Here, there were claims of 'hysteria' in the bar that day. This is an unjustified and exaggerated description of what happened. In non-clinical terms, hysteria is behaviour that exhibits overwhelming or unmanageable fears. There was absolutely nothing indicating overwhelming fear. A barmaid tells McKenna who Bailey is, and some people clap when he leaves the bar. Neither are the actions of people experiencing a spike in fear.

A barmaid shares gossip about someone leaving the bar. This should be no surprise. That people in the bar celebrate when a bullying braggart leaves the premises is hardly resentment. The idea that this caused McKenna to take time out of his holiday to lie to Police Officers is preposterous.

The second attempt to discredit McKenna is to point out that he did not immediately tell his wife about the confessions. This verges on the side of desperation. The delay in question was not several hours or days. It was a matter of minutes. They were still in the bar when he told his wife, and it was just after Bailey left.

One might as easily conclude that James McKenna might wait until Bailey left before telling his wife what had happened. This is far from 'notable' behaviour.

> "It is notable that James McKenna only told his wife what Bailey had allegedly said after he had witnessed the highly unusual demonstration of resentment by way of clapping,"

Mr Sheehan is not there to second-guess what was running through Mr McKenna's mind. He appears to have no talent for mind reading, and his remit is to stick to the facts.

When writing about the McKenna confession, The report states, 'This demonstrates hysteria and resentment against Bailey.' That is but one interpretation. There can be many others. For example, it could demonstrate that Bailey was known as a violent, obnoxious man – known to beat up Jules – and people believed he may have done the crime. They may have arrived at that conclusion based on known facts rather than the patronising suggestion of 'hysteria". We should remind ourselves that we know of at least 12 confessions made in front of 18 people. There may be more that were never reported. If others heard about Bailey's frequent confessions, they might take him at his word. This is a more plausible inference than 'mass hysteria'.

If the DPP report 'cherry-picked' explanations that supported its narrative while having no more or even less evidence to support its options, then it did a great disservice to Sophie's family. There is still time for the DPP to explain the evidential basis for this and other opinions found throughout the report.

The report author also inferred that because McKenna did not appear uncomfortable or jump up and walk away from Bailey, it somehow implies that Bailey did not confess. This is clutching at straws. Desperately so. One could argue that McKenna froze and was in shock for a short while. Or McKenna could have decided to be stoic and not take any sudden actions with a man who has just said he murdered a woman. The truth is we don't know what lay beneath McKenna's behaviour. Sheehan was there to be a professional lawyer, not an amateur, long-distance psychologist.

Given the importance of confessions, McKenna was interviewed for a second time in greater detail. This results in an outrageous evidence-free accusation in the DPP report:

> "It is particularly notable that James McKenna in his second statement in order to amplify the alleged seriousness of the admission and the consequent shock he suffered as a result of hearing it, says that he cannot recall the invitation to visit the Thomas home." (to have drinks with Bailey and Thomas)

This was one more negative assumption about anything that points to Bailey being culpable for the murder. The suggestion was McKenna was trying to amplify the alleged seriousness of what happened. This is pure speculation, an evidence-free hunch. No evidence is produced to show McKenna was seeking to amplify anything. One must wonder why the report's author kept making assumptions that undermined people who made statements that pointed to Bailey's guilt. The report fails to give a single logical reason for doubting a tourist taking the time to make a statement to investigators. It would have been easier for McKenna to have done nothing but he acted.

The report highlights inconsistencies between Mr. and Mrs. McKenna and between James McKenna's first and second statements. These were concerning broader topics. The central issue of the Bailey confession has remained unchanged.

The conclusion of the review of the McKenna evidence reduces the report to high farce. It states Sheehan's point of view and that of the senior officers of the DPP. McKenna is deemed unreliable because there is inconsistency between his statements and between him and his wife. The issue here is not about McKenna. It is the rank hypocrisy and double standards of the report. There are countless examples of Bailey being inconsistent and lying. There are also many significant inconsistencies between Bailey and Jules Thomas. Despite this and much more, the DPP does not suggest that Bailey cannot be believed.

> "It is clear that McKenna's second statement cannot be relied on. It is not consistent with his first statement and conflicts with the statement of his wife."

It is impossible to read that comment from the report and not be mystified by the biases and thought processes that led the author to question the veracity of McKenna's statements while saying nothing about Bailey's conduct. Once the questionable assumptions are ignored, there are insufficient grounds to reject Mckenna's evidence.

The Shelleys

> "Ian Bailey came into the kitchen and cried "I did it", repeating this about four or five times"
>
> "I went too far, I went too far"
>
> From a statement made by Richard Shelley

The final confession included in the DPP report was the one made to the Shelleys. After meeting Bailey and Thomas in a bar they went back to the Prairie cottage to continue to drink and socialise. There, in a drunken and emotional state,

Bailey confessed to the murder of Sophie. The report utilised some typical tropes to challenge an anti-Bailey statement.

> "the community had been exhorted to obtain incriminating evidence in the matter."

The first technique is to claim that the people giving anti-Bailey statements are in some way being 'coerced' and pressurised into making their statements. The phrasing of this comment is rather unusual. It appears as if it is suggesting that someone (AGS?) is putting pressure on people to come up with evidence that incriminates Bailey. It was almost as if the DPP were hinting that people may be encouraged by the police to fabricate evidence. If that were true it would be appalling. If the report was suggesting that people were being encouraged to provide genuine evidence that may help to catch the murderer, that would be a good idea. It would have been helpful if the DPP had been less ambiguous on the subject. If the author was hinting at something nefarious, then he should have put up tangible evidence or refrained from such gossip.

> "An objective assessment of the alleged conversation between Richie Shelley and Ian Bailey does not demonstrate that the conversation was about the murder."

The report refers to an objective assessment. In this context 'objective' means the assessment from a Dublin office is correct, and Shelley's was wrong. The use of the word objective attempts to give an opinion a veneer of authority. It does not do so. The Shelleys were there; they knew what they experienced and what they understood. Once again, the author decides he knows what happened better than those who were there. Every time he presumes to know better, it favours Ian Bailey.

> "It is, however, a matter of indisputable fact that Bailey has consistently and publicly proclaimed his innocence on other occasions."

Proclamations of innocence often tend to be public, and confessions tend to be private. That has no bearing on what happened that night. It does not mean Bailey did not confess. The truth of that assertion depends upon his definition of 'public.' If the public included confessing in front of 2 or 3 people, then he is wrong. Bailey confessed to two people (once) and three people (twice). The reference to these confessions in front of more than one person may surprise people reading the report, as the author saw fit to exclude all of those confessions without any explanation.

The DPP said that the Shelleys' delay in coming forward, which lasted a couple of years, makes their evidence less credible and unworthy of consideration. This is not a convincing inference, as there are other potential explanations. There was no written policy at the DPP that statements not made immediately would be routinely rejected.

> "If the alleged conversation took place he did not attach sufficient weight to it to even bother reporting it."

The comment about Shelley not attaching sufficient weight is an opinion based on scant evidence. The DPP report is there to weigh actual evidence, not to promote the author's views. While opinions with little or no basis, in fact, are plentiful, the report never prefers an opinion indicating Bailey's guilt.

The report concluded that the Shelley's evidence was dangerously unreliable. There is little in what was written to justify such a startling conclusion.

> "On an overall basis the Shelley evidence is dangerously unreliable"

The DPP's thoughts on these confessions implied that the people who made their reports lacked social and emotional skills and could not interpret what Bailey was saying. The popular theme was that statements were not made within an unspecified timescale. If there were doubts, then those people should have their evidence tested in a witness box. Instead, the DPP years later decided that they knew best and they would side with Ian Bailey. They had, of course, failed to identify his lies. None of these people reporting confessions had the slightest incentive to lie about their experiences, whereas Bailey had lied dozens of times to AGS.

So far, the focus has been on the failures of the DPP to adequately analyse the confessions included in the report. The report also fails the victims of this crime and people seeking justice by the way so much evidence was excluded. There are at least seven further confessions by Ian Bailey, These further confessions were witnessed by twelve people.

In two cases, three people witnessed a confession. The confession to three people in the Barrett home was made on the same day as the confession made to Yvonne Ungerer. The content of the Barrett home confession was a close match for the one reported by Bill Hogan.. These commonalities are corroborative. They are all excluded. Not only were they left out, but there was no explanation why the DPP had decided to do so. If the twelve statements and seven confessions that were excluded were flawed, then the DPP should have put in the time and effort to explain the exclusions.

People from all walks of life in a variety of social situations and with no axe to grind regarding Bailey say that he confessed. There is no evidence that they lied or had cognitive impairments or psychiatric disorders.

The totality of the confession evidence is another strong indicator that Ian Bailey murdered Sophie.

The seven excluded statements on scratches are now joined by the exclusion of twelve statements on confessions.

For statements, see Appendix 2: pt 9

Ian Bailey's alleged prior knowledge of Sophie Toscan Du Plantier (Report section 2)

When writing about Bailey's prior knowledge of Sophie, the DPP report first explains Bailey conceded that he once saw Sophie at a distance in the summer of 1995. It then goes on to the call from Eddie Cassidy, which Bailey received at 1.40 pm on December 23rd. What is interesting both here and elsewhere is that the report quotes Bailey with no caveats. Bailey claims he was asked about Toormore, and he was told a French woman had been murdered. The report asserts Bailey steadfastly denies knowing Sophie. However, the assertions of a liar, if uncorroborated, have little value. For this reason, one would expect the DPP to seek out other sources of evidence that may inform us whether Bailey knew Sophie. There are plenty in the files. Alas, this search does not appear to have be done with any rigour, if at all.

The report concludes that "The Garda contention that Bailey is being untruthful and evasive regarding his knowledge of Sophie Toscan du Plantier is not supported by convincing evidence." After reading what was written in the report it would be reasonable to agree with this final conclusion. There appeared to be no evidence. However, if one digs into the findings of AGS, the evidence is not as the report suggests. Let us dig deeper.

In chapters 2,3 and 4 of this book, it was shown that Bailey knew a huge amount about Sophie on the day she died. She was not a stranger to him. He knew who she was, where she lived, that she was in Dreenane at the time, he knew she was alone, and he knew exactly where he would find her dead body. For reasons unknown the DPP made no reference to any of this nor to the dozens of independent statements that showed it to be the case.

In chapter nine the evidence from nine statements all showing that Bailey knew Sophie were presented. All this evidence was ignored in the report. If every single piece of evidence showing that Bailey knew Sophie is excluded, then it is hardly surprising that the DPP claims Bailey did not know her. This is outrageous.

If the author believed every one of those admissions to knowing Sophie was untrue, he ought to have explained the reasons for his conclusions. To leave out those statements without explanation was unconscionable. The report repeatedly excluded evidence that showed Bailey to be culpable regarding the murder.

For statements, see Appendix 2: pt 10

Conclusion

When all the evidence is considered, there are compelling reasons to charge Bailey and have the evidence tested in a trial. Bailey had few or no scratches or other injuries when he left the Galley bar on the night of December 22nd. At least some, possibly all, of the confessions were true, and Ian Bailey knew Sophie Toscan du Plantier far better than he had admitted publicly.

The remaining questions are why so many pro-Bailey assumptions were found in these sections of the report and why dozens of statements condemning Bailey were excluded. How could the DPP justify ignoring seven important statements on scratches, twelve on confessions, and nine on Bailey knowing Sophie? What approach results in 28 statements being ignored?

CHAPTER **14**

Bailey's alleged incriminating knowledge of the murder (Report section 11)

This section of the report contains an appalling factual error that will most likely have caused considerable pain to Sophie's family. It is a shameful error that is so bad that it makes it impossible to take the report seriously. The DPP report boldly stated, "The body of Sophie Toscan Du Plantier was found by Alfie Lyons at 10.10 a.m. on 23 December 1996". This is the description of the discovery of a woman brutally battered to death in a frenzied attack. In that single sentence are two unforgivable errors. How often did the author draft, read, and re-draft the report? How many times did others fact-check it? How often did senior DPP members read through and endorse the report? For a report of such importance, one would expect the directors to have gone through the final version with a fine tooth comb. Yet the sentence gets the time of discovery wrong, and the name of the person discovering the dead woman is also wrong. It should have read: The body of Sophie Toscan Du Plantier was found by Shirley Foster at 10 a.m. on 23 December 1996.

These were two basic facts about the case. To call this sloppy would be too kind. It is incompetent. One can hardly be surprised that this report fails to grasp the importance of dozens of key statements when the organisation cannot get the most basic facts right. One may also wonder what professional standards and guidelines would allow this nonsense to be approved. At the risk of digressing, we should imagine how this factual ineptitude impacted on the family and friends of Sophie Toscan du Plantier. There appears to be no evidence that the directors of the DPP or Robert Sheehan had the good grace to apologise for this incompetence.

In this section, as in many others, the report author devotes much of his energy to trying to show Bailey was a wronged man while ignoring statements that perfectly spelled out what happened.

Sheehan's problem on this topic was that he had a blind spot. He has bought the Bailey lie that he found out about the death of a French woman in Dreenane from Cassidy. He should not be embarrassed by his error. It has been shared by many. However, they did not have all the statements. The DPP did but failed to see the truth.

The report author appears to have convinced himself that Bailey was telling the truth about what Cassidy told him on the afternoon of 23.12.1996. Imagine that. Bailey was a pathological liar who was repeatedly caught in lies, yet Sheehan believed everything he said. This was such a folly. To believe this narrative, Cassidy needed to have all the information about the murder at the time he called Bailey.

This would result in the creation of a whole new narrative — one that had no basis, in fact, a work of fiction.

The DPP narrative about incriminating knowledge requires that one or more people provide Cassidy with all the relevant information about the death. In that way, he could pass it on to Bailey, turning Bailey into the innocent recipient of all the inside information.

From Twomey's mouth to Bailey's ears: The 'DPP' version

1. Twomey told Cassidy that a French woman had been murdered in Dreenane

2. Cassidy passed this information on to Bailey

3. Bailey then knew there was a murdered French woman in Dreenane

It is a simple three-step process. The DPP kept this theory in the report. In this section, much was written about the timing and duration of calls. The report fails to produce evidence of this flow of information. Unable to find one jot of evidence to support the theory, Mr Sheehan writes:

"I can see no reason why Superintendent Twomey would not have told Cassidy that the deceased was French and that she had been murdered."

He believed that because he could not see a reason, it must not exist, a bizarre conclusion. His whole theory is based on an uncorroborated assumption.

The reader of this report may assume it eliminated alternative scenarios. If it did, they remain a secret. Those people who are not hard of thinking may be able to enumerate several reasons why a senior police officer may not tell a journalist detailed information about a recent crime. One reason would be professional ethics. Superintendent Twomey may believe in protecting confidential information. This is obviously not an option the report subscribed to. Not only does Sheehan think Twomey gave confidential information to Cassidy, he also believes that Twomey lied in his statements when he said he did no such thing.

Another reason that Twomey would refrain from disclosing everything to Cassidy is the importance of not disclosing information vital to the case, especially as this was so soon after Shirley Foster discovered the crime. Twomey may have refrained from blurting everything out until all facts were checked and double-checked. It may be reasonable to expect a Superintendent would want that done first. A senior officer would tend to be guarded in declaring a suspicious death as murder, this is another reason the report failed to address. One further reason Twomey is unlikely to give Cassidy such details is out of respect for the victim's family, whoever she might turn out to be. He might reasonably want her family to be informed before sharing what he may have known.

There will be other reasons for Twomey not telling Cassidy the details. Alas, the report did not suggest any of them. For the DPP, it had to be Twomey telling Cassidy. This meant those two people must have lied in their statements to AGS. The police and the press were to blame. Ian Bailey was the victim. Without the fact-free assumption that the two men were liars, the house of cards collapses, and rightly so.

The DPP would need to do more than rely on a false premise to make their scenario work. It would have to ignore and exclude facts that demonstrated the scenario was a groundless waste of time. The DPP would have to ignore inconvenient facts.

Ian Bailey was not so special

For the DPP tale to be plausible, we are asked to believe that Ian Bailey had a special place in Eddie Cassidy's heart and mind. This was nonsensical. They hardly knew each other. Bailey was one of many freelancers that Cassidy would have on his 'Rolodex'. He would be the stringer living closest to the scene of the incident. Many other Cassidy contacts would be long-established and people he would trust. Some were likely to be personal friends.

Cassidy called several newspaper people around the time he called Bailey. Yet he did not mention a murdered French woman in the Dreenane area to any of them. Not one. Can anyone accept the proposition that the information went from Twomey's mouth to Bailey's ears alone? For the DPP theory to be believed, people must accept that Cassidy shared his scoop only with a freelancer he did not know well while withholding information from tried and tested long-term colleagues. There was no evidence of a special relationship between Cassidy and Bailey. This is because no such relationship existed. For the DPP narrative to be plausible, people had to believe Cassidy considered Bailey to be unique. This was a theory that appeared to be little more than a hunch.

The reality is that Twomey had many reasons not to tell Cassidy everything. There is no evidence that such information was shared nor any evidence to support the insinuation that Twomey and Cassidy were liars. There is nothing in the relationship between Cassidy and Bailey to suggest that Cassidy would share everything with Bailey and share little or nothing with everyone else.

The DPP is defeated by its own 'logic'

Elsewhere, Sheehan asks why Bailey did nothing if he knew about the crime earlier. The answer is simple. First, Bailey could not go public until he was formally told about the murder. Second, as we will soon see, he did many things in private regarding the crime in the hours leading up to the Cassidy call.

Why did Sheehan not apply the same rationale to Cassidy? If Cassidy knew the details of a murder, why did he not take immediate action? That was his job as a newspaperman. If he had reliable sources at noon telling him there was a murdered French woman in Dreenane, why did he wait 90 minutes before he started taking action? He had nothing to hide. If he had access to confidential information early, that would be a 'feather in his cap.'

The DPP offers no explanation for why Cassidy did nothing for well over an hour, and when he took action, his priority was giving all his confidential information to a jobbing freelancer he hardly knew. Do they have evidence of Cassidy calling relevant people from 12 pm? It's a rhetorical question. He called no one about the deceased woman at that time because he did not know at that time. No evidence supports the 'Twomey, Cassidy, Bailey' scenario because it did not happen. The hypothesis was, and is a dud.

While Cassidy was doing nothing, chapter three showed that Bailey and Thomas were very active.

Cassidy does somersaults

The report expected readers to believe that Cassidy 'sat on his scoop' for up to 90 minutes telling no one, and when he got around to acting, he told only Ian Bailey the full story. Even this farrago is not the full extent of the nonsense the DPP expected readers to swallow in this case.

By its logic, the report said Cassidy had the inside track and ran with it but then chose to deny it. Why would a journalist have valuable information on the location, nationality, and cause of death, share it only with Bailey, and then repeatedly deny knowing such things in police statements? This would mean that instead of rejoicing at his success, Cassidy would suddenly pretend it had never happened. It is patent nonsense.

If Cassidy had told Bailey the victim was a murdered French woman, why would he then go on to deny it? In his statements, he said that at the time of speaking to Bailey, he did not know the victim had been murdered nor that she was French. If he got the information from a confidential source, he would use it while protecting that source. Telling only Bailey and then denying it in the years to follow makes no sense. The DPP narrative is found wanting yet again

This is what happens when an evidence-free hypothesis based on a groundless assumption is tested by logic and evidence, It falls to pieces. There is evidence from one further person that highlights the ludicrous nature of the DPP version that defends Bailey. That person is Ian Bailey!

The tale of the missing evidence

The now eviscerated DPP theory had suggested that Bailey knew the deceased woman was murdered, French, and she lived in Dreenane. The information allegedly went to Bailey from Superintendent Twomey via Eddie Cassidy. The DPP implied that Bailey did not have guilty knowledge; he simply received inside information.

The challenge for the DPP theory of how Bailey got his information is that he completely changed his story between 1996 and 1998.

The 1998 version is a very different story compared with 1996 and 1997. There is no mention of a murder. The deceased woman is twice referred to as a non-national with an equivocating reference to her being French. Prior to this, Bailey was insistent that the victim was French. In the 1998 version, Bailey no longer meets Foster on Dreenane Lane as he drives to the cottages at the end of that lane. He now says he met her at the junction, and Foster directs Bailey down the lane. The DPP neither acknowledged nor explained how their theory of how Bailey knew about the case accounts for the total changes in Bailey's narrative. They failed to specify what exactly went from Twomey's lips to Bailey's ears.

The theory of what Bailey was told about the death and how he was informed is in tatters. This is because all the evidence showing Bailey knew about the murder many hours before the Cassidy call was excluded from the report.

The facts and statements in chapter three highlight this foolhardy escapade. Bailey knew the information before the Gards even arrived in Dreenane. He knew because he murdered Sophie. The statements show it to be so. The 'Twomey, Cassidy, Bailey theory' is an embarrassment.

By ignoring the statements and creating an evidence-free theory, The DPP report did Sophie, her family, and Justice a disservice,

For statements, see Appendix 2: pt 4

CHAPTER **15**

Alleged similar fact evidence and sexual motive (Report section 15)

The DPP section on similar fact evidence and sexual motives is yet another mishmash of snippets of information. Some of it is potentially relevant, with other parts appearing as bizarre inclusions. The first part of the DPP report on this subject opens with Jules Thomas's views on Ian Bailey's violence. It is unclear why this was deemed relevant. She minimises the violence visited on her by Bailey, and the report thought it important for readers to know that Thomas thought her previous partner was a worse individual who kicked her while wearing hobnail boots. One thing she does say more than once is that Bailey is prone to violence when he has been drinking. Here was a potential example of similar fact evidence yet the DPP did not highlight it. Likewise, there are references to Bailey promising to desist from the violence and then repeating his assaults. A man lacking self-control regarding his violent outbursts. The report fails to highlight something that works against Bailey.

With reference to the law, similar fact evidence is presented to establish the conditions under which factual evidence of past misconduct of the accused can be admitted at trial to infer that the accused committed the misconduct at issue. The DPP reasoned that the beatings of Jules Thomas did not constitute similar facts with respect to the murder of Sophie Toscan du Plantier. The report states:

> "The principal assault on Jules Thomas did not require her to be detained in hospital. It related to a domestic incident and unfortunately such violence is not uncommon."

The first three words there are telling. What they tell us is that the assault was not a one-off event. There are others, of which the report focussed on the principal example. However, the author chooses not to present the history of Bailey's violent conduct. It is not the only thing he excludes. He then offers a brief reference to this principal violent outburst, pointing out that Thomas did not stay overnight in the hospital. This smacks of trying to minimise the ferocity of the attack. In this chapter, you will learn the whole story. The one the DPP failed to present in the report.

Before we look at the assault in question, the second half of the quote ought to be unpicked. The report says, 'It related to a domestic incident, and unfortunately, such violence is not uncommon.' It is never explained why violence being 'domestic' is somehow decidedly different from non-domestic violence. Nor does it explain why many men beating their partners is in some way different from other violence against

Alleged similar fact evidence and sexual motive (Report section 15)   259

women. The phraseology is more akin to old-fashioned views in 1901, not 2001.

Having said the worst assault perpetrated by Bailey did not require hospital detention, it is then then contrasted with the murder of Sophie. In that case, he is less reticent in describing what happened. This puts a greater distance between the two violent attacks. With that distance comes the implication that there can be no similar facts of interest.

> "What is uncommon is the brutal form of murder of Sophie Toscan du Plantier whereby she suffered the infliction of approximately 50 wounds. The killing of Sophie Toscan du Plantier is not similar to the domestic violence in relation to Jules Thomas. "

Let's see what the report left out. The principal assault was a savage and sustained beating. The assault took place seven months before the murder. It was done by a 6' 3" man, a former rugby player, to a much smaller, physically weaker, and older woman. A description of her injuries on the night of the beating was heard in evidence in a 2003 case. Though the case came after the report, the events were well-known in 2001. This is how the neighbour of Jules Thomas described the scene when he went to the cottage on the night of the beating. He had gone to the house at the behest of the daughters. When they asked Bailey for the car keys so they could take their mother to the hospital, he refused to hand them over and screamed at them.

> Peter Bielecki
>
> "I could hear what I can only describe as animal sounds of terrible distress. Jules was curled up at the end of the bed in foetal position. Her hair was completely tousled and large clumps of her hair were missing, she had clumps of hair in her hand and her eye was purple. It was huge; a pink fluid was dripping from it and her mouth was swollen. Her face had gouges on it, her right hand had bite marks on it. It was like the soul, the spirit, had gone out of her. It was the most appalling thing I have ever witnessed."

There are photographs taken of Thomas after her severe beating. Her left eye had swelled so big that it has been described as being like a grapefruit. It was certainly heavily swollen. There were sizeable bald patches on her head where large clumps of hair had been ripped away. We know there were also bite marks on Thomas, and her lip had been torn away from her mouth. This was a savage attack by a large drunken man who was out of control. Bailey inflicted those injuries on a woman he professed to love.

The assault on Thomas was a sustained drunken attack with a significant focus on the head. This was true of Sophie Toscan du Plantier. There was rage and 'overkill' in both cases. A single punch would have hurt and incapacitated Thomas. The repeated punches to her face, biting, and ripping her hair out are indicative of a man out of control. There was no doubt that Bailey had hit her many times.

Why did the DPP exclude all of this? If the true extent of her injuries were included, could any reasonable person suggest there were no similar facts? Why this information was left out is not known. However, it fits the pattern of the repeated exclusion of evidence that indicates Bailey's guilt.

His personal diaries and journals were damning yet they were left out of the report. Bailey wrote the following:

> "of late since Easter I have on a number of occasions struck and abused my lover the thing I believe is the worst crime a man can commit against one's own mother's sex. I know that each time has been over drink"

Between Easter Sunday, April 7th, and Bailey recording that information was a matter of a few weeks. In a few weeks, he had 'struck and abused' Thomas on many occasions. This portrays a man who readily and repeatedly used violence. He attributed the violence to drink. Despite knowing the impact of drinking heavily, he continued to do so almost nightly. If this omission was not bad enough, worse entries were overlooked. Such as:

> "I attacked and severely beat Jules to such an extent that she required hospital treatment, when on reaching the house I relived the attack and proceeded to cause further injury on top. I felt a sense of sickness at seeing my own account of that dreadful night I actually tried to kill her."

Bailey reveals that the attack was sustained. It started while the couple were out, and then when they got home, the beating continued. This level of aggression should not have been overlooked. Then he writes, 'I actually tried to kill her.' For some reason, Ian Bailey confessing to his murderous intent does not warrant even a mention. The information was provided by AGS but played no part in the report. In fairness, it appears that Bailey could confess with impunity.

In a 2003-4 civil case instigated by Bailey versus eight newspapers, the overwhelming majority of the evidence heard by Justice Moran was known to the DPP in 2001. He took a different view of the facts about Bailey. The judge stated.

> "The question of violence towards women is a fact. What came across as a result of questions from Mr Gallagher is that Ms Thomas suffered three nasty assaults. Mr Bailey appeared in the District Court over one of those and received a suspended sentence. Mr Bailey says that when he was violent, it takes place domestically [sic] and is a domestic problem. I deal with a lot of family law in this court. One rarely comes across instances of beatings. In this case we have three. Violence once would be unusual. Violence twice would be unusual. Three times is exceptional. The District Court gave a six-month suspended sentence because his partner said she forgave him. Otherwise, the District judge would have had no hesitation in imposing a custodial sentence. I certainly have no hesitation in describing Mr Bailey as a violent man and I think the defendants have no problem in describing him as violent towards women, plural."

The case, as presented in the report, says there was no similar fact evidence. However, when the full facts are presented, the case against Bailey is far stronger. There can be no question that the 'principal' assault was severe, yet the DPP report downplayed the extent of the injuries by failing to describe them. The writings of Bailey show him to be a dangerous man. The common ground between Thomas and du Plantier includes attacks focused on women, heavy drinking, and rage. Extreme and excessive violence with a significant inclination to repeatedly attack the head, continuing to rain blows on the victim long after they are incapacitated. One must ask why the report flagrantly excluded similar facts. It was an unforgivable omission.

Sexual motives

Any exploration of Ian Bailey's sexual motives and motivations should reasonably include a study of his diaries and journals. These were available to the DPP. They show a man with a lifelong obsession with hard-core pornography and hard-core sex. His writings included entries stating he enjoyed watching pornography in which three men had sex with one little girl. That is paedophilia and child rape. In another entry, he described how he wanted sex with a 14-year-old girl and her friends. There were many descriptions of hard-core sex. There was at least one recording of him talking about rape. Not a word of this is mentioned in the report.

Instead, the report focuses on two cases of highly inappropriate sexual behaviour. One took place on the properties owned by the Thomas family. The other took place at a party. The way these cases are characterised in the report is shocking and leaves much to be desired.

The first case involved a young woman called Collette Gallagher. She had been at the Thomas cottage drinking with Bailey and Jules Thomas. She was offered somewhere to sleep for the night. Gallagher was to stay at the Studio. You will remember that the DPP stated that the cottage and the studio were adjacent when they were a long way apart. In the early hours of the morning. Bailey left the cottage and took the three-minute, 200-metre walk to the Studio. He went there intending to have sex with Gallagher while there was no indication that she was interested in him. He went to her bedroom, undressed, and then got into bed with her without her consent. Then he started to make intimate contact with her also without her consent.

Any further sexual assault was prevented when Jules Thomas turned up at the studio. The report stated the opinion that it was an overstatement that this was attempted rape. Maybe the DPP believed Bailey would stroke her leg and then return to the cottage had Thomas not appeared. What it does show is a man who sneaked out of the cottage when he thought his partner was asleep to go somewhere where he expected to have sex. A man who would initiate intimate sexual activity despite there being zero indication of consent. A man who thought he had the right to treat a woman in such a vile way. To downplay this behaviour by saying it is not attempted rape is unacceptable from a public

Alleged similar fact evidence and sexual motive (Report section 15) 265

servant. This was inappropriate sexual behaviour without any attempt to establish consent.

In the Leftwick case, there was an evening birthday party with alcohol readily available. In his late thirties, Bailey decided he would pick up a 15-year-old girl – with only the two of them in the room – and ask the girl to wrap her legs around him. Once again, uncouth and disrespectful behaviour with a female. He did not attempt to get consent before grabbing the girl.

Robert Sheehan dismisses the suggestion that such behaviour was a sexual assault. He wrote it 'was a flirtatious act on the part of Bailey'. Not only did he write that, the DPP supported the statement. An older man grabbing a child and making that suggestion was flirting in the author's world. That offers insights into his mindset. It is despicable. Bailey can be seen as a man drunkenly acting in a gross, antisocial, and threatening manner.

Concerning Sophie Toscan du Plantier's murder, the report states there is no evidence of a sexual assault. This is different from saying there was not any sexually inappropriate or threatening behaviour. In the absence of evidence, we do not know. The cases of Gallagher and Leftwick both show us that a man can be sexually inappropriate without leaving physical evidence of a sexual assault. And Bailey was such a man.

There is a huge irony when Sheehan writes, 'References in the Garda Report to a sexual motive are pure speculation.' His was a report riven with assumptions and speculation. At the time of writing, there is no hard evidence to prove a sexual motive was involved. The downplaying of gross sexual inappropriateness regarding Gallagher and Leftwick, the comments about domestic violence, and the avoidance of spelling out the violence meted out to Thomas all suggest some regrettable out-of-touch attitudes toward women.

In terms of similar fact evidence, there is a case to be made for it when the full facts are considered. There are themes of drinking linked to disinhibition. and disinhibition, leading to Bailey behaving in an immoral and illegal way. Whether it be inappropriate sexual conduct or violence, in the case of Thomas and Sophie Toscan du Plantier, the victims are always girls or women.

The similar fact evidence was not identified because the DPP excluded so much relevant evidence. Only they know why they chose to do that.

When all the facts are presented rather than excluded, a strong case can be made that there was similar fact evidence between the severe beating of Thomas and Toscan du Plantier.

Case Closed

In parts one and two of this book, the case against Ian Bailey was presented. There can be no doubt that he murdered Sophie Toscan du Plantier. There is a combination of his lies about the murder and the things he knew that only the murderer or someone close to the murderer could know. The dozens of statements given independently by trustworthy sources made the case compelling. It is little wonder that the French judges found Bailey guilty in 2019.

Despite the wealth of evidence, the DPP concluded that 'A prosecution against Bailey is not warranted by the evidence '. This was an extraordinary outcome. It raised the question of how the DPP could conclude there was insufficient evidence while at the same time choosing to exclude so much.

Robert Sheehan had virtually all the information described in parts one and two of this book. This begs the question of how the DPP reached its 2001 conclusion.

Baseless assumptions, weird theories, and other hokum

The report frequently presented assumptions or inferences not supported by the facts. The case made in support of Bailey is littered with fact-free opinions. There are sixteen examples of this in Appendix 3. The report repeatedly rejects evidence based solely on when the statements were taken. Conclusions are reached about what people were thinking or feeling without any evidence. The author thought he knew what was said and the way it was said better than people who were present at the time. On no less than four occasions, the report said the arrest of Thomas was unlawful when it was not. There were errors made on crucial facts and information that had no bearing on the case was included. The information on Bruno Carbonnet and Jules Thomas being kicked by a former partner are two examples.

A fixation on AGS took up far too much of the report and had little bearing on whether Bailey should or should not be charged. And who can forget the hoops the DPP jumped through to say that Bailey's knowledge of the crime came from Superintendent Twomey? To make this tale stand up, it became necessary to assume a senior journalist and a senior police officer were bare-faced liars.

It was a bizarre assemblage of random thoughts

Ignoring and failing to analyse evidence

The report omitted all the lies told by Ian Bailey. It did not analyse his ever-changing story. The false alibi was minimised to virtually nothing, and the stark differences between the 1996 and 1998 statements were ignored.

The statements that went unanalysed, mainly ignored, or completely excluded, can be found in Appendix 2. These include the exclusion of Bailey's lies about the night of December 21st (point1 - 8 statements), the changing tale of the journey home on the 22nd (point 2 – 4 statements), the failure to analyse Bailey's ever-changing story regarding the morning of the 23rd (point 3 – 5 statements). A total of seventeen statements. When these statements are ignored, it becomes very easy to conclude that Bailey made a few errors rather than systematically lied. This is what happened in the 2001 report. If all Bailey's statements were scrutinised there could have been only one conclusion. Ian Bailey repeatedly lied to investigators.

Excluding dozens of key witnesses and their statements

In parts one and two of this book, the case against Bailey was made. The 2001 report missed out on the whole narrative, indicating Bailey's guilt. This included 7 statements about the absence of injuries in the Galley Bar (Appendix 2: point 8 – 7 statements). Bailey knew about the murder from very early on the 23rd, long before his phone call from Eddie Cassidy (point 4b – 10 statements and point 5 – 4 statements). Likewise, there was the failure to deal with Bailey changing his story about going to Dreenane (point 6 – 5 statements) and changing his reason for going to the Post Office (point 7 – 5 statements). To top this off the DPP made no mention of twelve statements concerning seven further confessions (point 9b – 12 statements), and they ignored the statements showing Bailey knew Sophie (point 10c – 9 statements). This is the entire case against Bailey, and it has been left out. The report can't be considered balanced when 52 statements making a compelling case against Bailey are excluded.

It is easy to conclude Bailey should not be charged when the case against him never sees the light of day. This is wholly unreasonable. The notion that 69 or more key statements were omitted and that this was acceptable to all the senior staff at the DPP is profoundly regrettable. These statements were made invisible, and the DPP did not explain why these people were ignored.

Why?

The notion that Bailey did not have a case to answer was untrue and led to decades of further suffering for a bereaved family. Only the people at the DPP know why they thought their report was acceptable. Maybe someday they may wish to explain what they did to Sophie's family and the Irish people. It is not too late to do so.

APPENDIX 1

The chronology of Ian Bailey's involvement in the Sophie Toscan du Plantier case

December 23rd, 1996: The battered dead body of Sophie Toscan du Plantier is found close to her home in Dreenane in Co Cork.

January 1997: Marie Farrell contacted gardaí saying she had seen a man acting suspiciously at Kealfadda Bridge, close to Sophie's home, in the early morning of December 23. She later identified the man as Ian Bailey, a local freelance reporter.

February 1997: Ian Bailey was arrested, questioned, and released without charge.

January 1998: Ian Bailey was re-arrested and released without charge.

December 2003/January 2004: Ian Bailey took a civil case against seven newspapers for linking him to the killing. He lost five of the actions. He won two, but these were not linked to Sophie but the claim he had assaulted his former wife.

October 2005: Marie Farrell suddenly withdrew her statements that she had seen Ian Bailey at Kealfadda Bridge. She claimed she had been pressurised into making them by gardaí.

July 2008: After a new investigation was set up in France, Sophie Toscan du Plantier's body was exhumed for a fresh autopsy. The investigation was headed up by Judge Patrick Gachon. Back in Ireland, the DPP recommended that no prosecution follow from the Garda probe into the withdrawal of Marie Farrell's statements.

March 2011: As the French investigation continued, a High Court ruling in Ireland cleared the way for Ian Bailey's extradition to France.

October 2011: French investigators interviewrd up to 30 people as part of their fresh probe.

November 2011: The Supreme Court heard an application by Ian Bailey for a fresh High Court hearing.

March 2012: The Supreme Court unanimously granted Bailey's appeal.

August 2013: After a successful civil case was brought in France by Sophie Toscan du Plantier's family, they were awarded damages of €150,000. Under French law, victims of crime can sue the state for damages.

March 2015: Ian Bailey was unsuccessful when he took a civil action against the State and gardaí. After a trial of over 60 days the Jury needed only two hours to reject the claims of

Bailey. During the trial Marie Farrell, Bailey's 'star witness' stormed out of the witness box while being cross examined.

January 2016: A new judge was appointed to oversee the French investigation, after Judge Gachon was promoted.

April 2018: An unsuccessful challenge was made by Ian Bailey in the French Supreme Court against French efforts to put him on trial for the murder.

August 2018: The Garda Síochána Ombudsman Commission found that there was no clear evidence of high-level corruption by gardaí investigating the murder. This showed Bailey's claims of corrupt and criminal behaviour by AGS were without merit

May 2019: A French trial in the absence of Ian Bailey got underway in Paris. It found him guilty in his absence and imposed a 25-year sentence.

October 2020: The High Court ruled that Mr Bailey would not be extradited to France. It was made clear that the decision was not based on Bailey's guilt or innocence.

April 2021: Mr Bailey and his long-term partner, Jules Thomas, split up after almost three decades together. She demanded that he leave her property.

June 2022: Gardaí announced a cold case review into the murder in Ireland.

December 2022: Gardaí held a press conference in Schull where they called for further witnesses to come forward to help their investigation. Officers said they wished to speak to any person who met, spoke with, or had any interaction with Ms du Plantier from when she arrived in Ireland on December 20, 1996, to when her body was discovered on the morning of December 23.

January 2024: Ian Bailey died. The cold case review continues.

APPENDIX 2:

Statements indicating Bailey's guilt, including over 60 excluded or severely minimised regarding the 2001 DPP report

"The DPP must act on evidence."
James Hamilton

1. The night of the 21ˢᵗ and the morning of the 22ⁿᵈ

The lies Bailey told about what he did on the evening of 21.12 1996 and the morning of 22.12.1996

I Bailey	31.12.96 Chopped down a Christmas tree with Saffron Thomas on the morning of the 22ⁿᵈ. Thus, at the Prairie that morning.
I Bailey	14.01.97 Went to the Courtyard with JT. No mention of her leaving early. Got up midday 22ⁿᵈ and killed the Turkeys with all the family present. No mention of staying the night in Schull.

P Murphy	15.01.97 Bailey in Schull
M Murphy	12.01.97 Bailey in Schull
A Doran	01.02.97 Bailey in Schull
R Shelly	11.01.97 Bailey in Schull
P Murphy	25.01.97 Bailey asked her if she told AGS he was there 21/22
I Bailey	10.02.97 Confirmed he was in Schull 21/22nd

8 statements

2. Journey home after 00 am on the 23.12.1996

The lies Bailey told about his journey home from the Galley bar

I Bailey	28.12.96 Courtyard pub until it closed then home with JT. No reference to route or stopping.
I Bailey	14.01.97 Did not return by Prairie route (most direct route) No reference to stopping
I Bailey	10.02.1997 72C Galley pub
I Bailey	10.02.1997 72D Stopped at Hunt's Hill

4 statements

3. Bailey repeatedly changed his story about what he did from 1 am to 1.40 pm on 23.12.1996

Bailey's minimum of 20 lies and falsehoods told to investigators between 1 am and 1.40 pm on 23.12.1996, including his false alibi

I Bailey 20 changes in what he did on the morning of the 23.12.1996	Statement 31.12.1996
1 change	Statement 10.02. 1997
11 changes	Statement 10.02. 1997
4 changes	Statement 27.01.1998
4 changes	Statement 27.01 1998

5 statements

4. The events on the morning of 23.12.1996, 8 am to 1 pm

The alternative narrative for the events for the actions if Ian Bailey and Jules Thomas between 1 am and 1 pm on 23.12.1996

4a Statements included in the 2001 DPP report

P O'Colmain	18.10.00
C. Leftwick	15.05.97

2 statements

4b Statements excluded by the 2001 DPP report

F Thomas	21.09.00 152G
B Fuller	20.02.97 Saw Thomas driving around 11 am alone Schull / Goleen Rd / Causeway
J Thomas	08.06.97 She was driving on the Causeway at 11 am spoke to Camier
D Cross	23.12.97 Bailey at SoC before cordoned off
M McSweeney	29.04.97 Bailey at SoC 10.30 am - 11.00 am
T McEnaney	03.04.97 Bailey missed the deadline and submitted the article after 4 pm
R Curran	24.02.97 Bailey missed the deadline and submitted the article after 4 pm
J Camier	21.09.98 Thomas says Bailey was in Dreenane investigating the murder of a French woman
S Thomas	01.04.2002 J Thomas tells Saffron about the murder at noon
D O'Sullivan	12.02.97 Sees Bailey and Thomas in car 12.20=30 approx

10 statements

5. The nationality of the deceased in the DPP report

Bailey's self-contradiction on the nationality of the victim was not addressed in the 2001 report, and evidence showing that Eddie Cassidy gave Bailey no information about the victim's nationality.

I Bailey	31.12.96 French lady – and again in1997
I Bailey	27.01.98 Non-national female possibly French
E Cassidy	12.02.97 He did not mention either nationality or murder and gave the location as Toormore
F Thomas	21.09.00 Bailey did not say the victim's nationality nor that she was murdered, and the location was somewhere near Schull

4 statements

6. Travelling to Dreenane

Bailey completely changed his story about how he found the crime scene. His original version was fully corroborated, while his later version(s) had no corroboration and was contradicted by Thomas and Foster.

I Bailey	31.12.96 drove directly to Dreenane Knew exactly where to go
J Thomas	10.02.97 Bailey said they would try Alfie's road, and they went straight there.

M Murrell	Statement 491 Thomas indicated to Detective Gda Murrell and other officers where she and Bailey met Foster down Dreenane lane not at the junction
S Foster	22.05.97 met Bailey and Jules on Dreenane Lane. Bailey told her he was there on official business
I Bailey	27.01.98 (G) met Foster at the junction of Dunmanus-Toormore Rd and Dreenane Rd she directed him to Dreenane

5 statements

7. Reason for going to the Post Office

Bailey completely changed his story concerning why he went to the Post Office. His original version was fully corroborated, while his later version(s) had no corroboration and was contradicted by Thomas Dukelow and Jermyn

I Bailey	31.12.96 Went to Post Office and got 'her name'
J Thomas	12.10.11 French investigation
A Dukelow	30.01.97
N Jermyn	09.05.97
I Bailey	27.01.98 (G) went to the Post Office "someone came up with the name of the French woman"

5 statements

8. Galley Bar / Scratches

The seven statements excluded or severely minimised by the DPP, which unanimously said Bailey had no injuries when he left The Galley bar around 00 am on 23.12.1996.

D Galvin	20.02.97
J McGowan	21.02.97
S Kelly	04.02.97
B Kelly	04.02.97
C Lynch	04.02.97
V. Galvin	21.02.97
P O'Regan	07.02.02

7 statements

9. Confessions

The twelve confessions given by Bailey and the eighteen people who witnessed them.

9a The six statements concerning 5 confessions included in the DPP report

Y Ungerer	11.07.97
H Callanan	10.02.97
M Reed	06.02.97
J McKenna	09.04.97
Richie Shelley	September 97
Rosie Shelley	04.09.97

9b The twelve statements concerning 7 confessions excluded from the DPP report

C Mangèz	08.07.97
B Fuller	20.02.97
B Fuller snr	01.07.97
M Fuller	01.07.97
B Hogan	January 1997, confirmed by Mr Hogan
R Barrett	Statement 251
C Deady	Statement 347
M Graham	25.02.97
Grant	23.08.97
Penney	17.01.99
O'Colmain	01.09.99
K Hendrick	28.04.02

12 statements

10. The 13 statements of witnesses showing that Bailey knew Sophie

10a The two included in the DPP report

A Lyons	22.05.97
Y Ungerer	11.02.97

10b The two that came after the DPP report

A Calahane	2012
P. Wilson	2012

10c The nine that were available, but the DPP chose to exclude them

P Webster	27.03.97
H Callanan	10.02.97
D Jackson	07.02.97
I Tullock	24/25.02.97
P Beirne	21.05.97
M Brown	30.01.97
J Kierans	27.02.97
C. Deady	10.02.97
M.Graham	18.02.97

9 statements

APPENDIX **3**

A sample of assumptions and assertions in the DPP 2001 report

"The DPP must act on evidence."
James Hamilton

In many places in the report, some assertions and assumptions appear to have little or no evidence to support them. Most of these comments have been highlighted in this book. A selection of 16 is presented here to give you a sense of just how much editorialising there is in a short 44-page report.

Even though the report was completed over twenty years ago, it would still be an act of decency if the DPP explained these comments, particularly as every single one of these statements is undeniably pro-Bailey. Without strong evidence for the assertions, the DPP might explain why they appeared in the report. The DPP appeared not to be acting on evidence

Comments made by Robert Sheehan and questions of evidence
"On tape Jules Thomas sounds credible and convincing."
What evidence did Mr Sheehan use to reach this conclusion? Thomas may sound that way to him, but that does not mean she is credible. Sheehan may be an inferior judge of audio evidence. Without knowing his expertise or the factual basis of what Thomas is saying, this type of judgment by Sheehan has no place in such a critical report.
S3 (section of the report)
"It is understood that the Gardaí issued similar warnings about Bailey to members of the community."
It is unclear what evidence Mr. Sheehan had to reach his 'understanding.' What were his sources? How did he quantify his data? Could he name the community members? Sophie Toscan du Plantier and her family deserve better than 'it is understood'.
S4

> "By inference, it seems that the O'Colmains are afraid that if they align themselves with Ian Bailey on any matter they will incur the disapproval of the Gardaí."
>
> 'By inference, it seems' is another vague evidence-free opinion of Mr Sheehan. Could different inferences be drawn? How precisely did Mr Sheehan measure and quantify levels of fear from his Dublin office? This comment smacks of Mr Sheehan 'mindreading' the O'Colmains. This is not the remit of a lawyer writing this type of report.
>
> S4

> "It might, for this reason, be thought that the unfortunate O'Colmains under such circumstances are most anxious to ingratiate themselves with the Gardaí and as such are witnesses of very little weight."
>
> Here, we have conjecture, not hard evidence. Without evidence, these conclusions may be shaped by Mr. Sheehan's cognitive biases. He concludes something 'might' be the case; he mindreads the emotional state of the O'Colmains and then concludes their evidence has very little weight based upon his evidence-free opinions.
>
> These are not reasonable, logical inferences drawn from the evidence; they are conclusions based on empty assumptions.
>
> S4

> **"On tape Bailey sounds credible and convincing."**
>
> When this report was written, it was evident from Bailey's statements that he had lied many times, including giving AGS a false alibi. Did Mr Sheehan consider the possibility that liars can sound 'credible and convincing'? Did Mr Sheehan listen to a range of recordings of Bailey before reaching a conclusion? Did Mr Sheehan have the humility to concede he might be a poor judge of recorded statements without access to non-verbal cues? How could such a judgment find its way into this report without more information?
>
> S4

> **"There has been a consistent flow of information to the media in relation to the investigation into the killing of Sophie Toscan Du Plantier."**
>
> A further statement of 'fact' that should have evidence to justify it. Once again, it resembles a mere opinion that may be prone to bias. What precisely was this 'consistent flow'? What was the nature and volume of this information? In any high-profile murder case, there will be a flow of information to the media. What were the examples of information flow that Mr Sheehan believed to be inappropriate?
>
> These vague assertions should not be part of a report of such importance.
>
> S4

> "Once Ian Bailey was believed by the public particularly in the local area to be responsible for the murder the fear thereby engendered was bound to create a climate in which witnesses became suggestible."
>
> This glib psychologising is shocking. There is unquantifiable public awareness said to lead to unquantifiable fear. This non-specific fear is then said to cause witnesses to become suggestible. This is flim-flam. It is bad enough in any discourse, but being used as the basis of a major legal decision makes it reprehensible. A heightened emotional state, even if it existed, might lead to people fleeing, forgetting, or simply becoming more resolute to tell the truth; the truth is we don't know if there was fear, and if there was fear, we do not know what it led to. The shocking truth is that Dublin office-based Robert Sheehan implies that he knows. Yet, he could not know.
>
> S4

"He states that the Gardaí were embarrassed by stories he had written, which indicated that they had no idea as to who had committed the murder. He had been told this by local people."

This is typical of the way the claims of Ian Bailey are presented uncritically. He claims to have been told things by anonymous 'people' or 'sources'. However, his stories are not checked and verified. What actual evidence was there that people said his stories were causing embarrassment? Why was the pathological liar believed? We know from parts one and two of this book that AGS had a very good idea that Bailey murdered Sophie. He did not like that so he created stories. Mr Sheehan bought what Bailey was selling. This type of statement underpinning a legal decision defies belief.

S4

> " He is also the Garda who would appear to have elicited incriminating observations against Bailey which Jules Thomas asserts were "Press Ganged" from her while she was unlawfully in custody."

Where to begin? A statement such as ' who would appear to have' is fact-free. It is an opinion with little or no substance. This is followed by a Thomas allegation of being 'press-ganged.' It ends with Sheehan's oft-repeated claim that Thomas was unlawfully in custody, which has never been found true by a single judge.

S8

> "It could certainly be argued that Oliver in an attempt to avoid a heavy sentence was anxious to please the Gardaí at the time of making the statement on 10 February 1998. Little if any incriminating weight can be attached to it."

Other explanations could be argued. What is required is evidence, not Sheehan's pro-Bailey theory. Without proof supporting his explanation, Sheehan concludes the evidence of Oliver has no weight. Based on an evidence-free theory, Sheehan writes of a person's evidence. This is a dire analysis.

S8

> "It is clear that Bailey was simply reciting what the Gardaí alleged to him while he was in custody."
>
> This is not clear; Ungerer was clear that Bailey was not reciting what someone else had said. He was admitting to a crime. Sheehan says he takes Bailey's side on this subject but has no tangible reason for doing so. Sheehan takes the word of a man who repeatedly lied to AGS over the evidence of a woman who had not. Sheehan should also have known that on the day this woman said Bailey had confessed to her, he also confessed differently to three men. Unfortunately, Sheehan excluded those three witness confessions from his report.
>
> Sheehan is reaching conclusions when he does not have the evidence to justify them.
>
> S9

> "It is abundantly clear that Malachi Reed was not upset by Ian Bailey on 4 February 1997, however, following his conversation with Gda. Kelleher he became upset and turned a conversation which had not apparently up until then alarmed him into something sinister.
>
> This is a further example of mind reading at the DPP. Here, a legal staffer in Dublin somehow knows the emotional state of a young man years earlier. The man who decided Ian Bailey was honest and reliable now claims to chart the level of upset of a young man he had never met. If this emotional projection were not so galling, it would be a high farce.
>
> [In 2003, Judge Horgan saw Reed give his evidence under oath and while being cross-examined and had no difficulty in concluding that Bailey confessed.]
> S9

> "When Helen Callanan refused to tell him he became frustrated and his remarks to her reek of sarcasm not veracity."

Helen Callanan was a successful journalist who went on to have a brilliant legal career. There is nothing to indicate that she has some cognitive impairment causing her to misunderstand the behaviour of a frustrated Ian Bailey. As in all the other cases, Robert Sheehan was not present. He could not hear Bailey's tone of voice or see his body language.

If he had done the analysis, he would have known 18 people witnessed 12 confessions, and he would have established that Bailey was a liar.

There is zero evidential basis for Sheehan to conclude 'his remark to her reek of sarcasm.' It should not be in a report of such importance.

Regrettably, the judge's comments in a high court case indicate that such strange conclusions were not unique.

S9

> "It is quite clear that Bailey wanted to find out who was slandering him."
>
> Slander –
>
> 'to damage someone›s reputation by making a false spoken statement about them'
>
> At this point, the report openly declares its partiality by stating that Ian Bailey was being slandered. The DPP does not say Bailey wanted to find out who was saying things he found offensive or objected to. No, the DPP says Bailey was being slandered. The DPP is saying that what is being said is false.
>
> Their mind was made up. This unfounded opinion clearly showed that the DPP would not let a trial test the facts.
>
> NB Bailey never won a legal case for slander or libel concerning what was said about his involvement in the murder case.
>
> S9

> "It is probable that many of these people told family, relations and friends."

This is more empty-headed speculation. If spreading information about the death happened, the DPP should provide concrete examples, evidence of which people they told, and an explanation or quantification of what 'probable' means in this context.

As it stood, it was an opinion dressed up as 'fact' — another example of an opinion being presented as objective truth.

S11

> "In a rural area the local grapevine can operate most efficiently."

This anecdotal observation has little or no point, and there is no reason to include it in this legal analysis. One could add statements such as: the local grapevine can fail to operate at all, can operate spasmodically, or communicate lies and rumours. There could be dozens of potential descriptors of local grapevines.

Yet Robert Sheehan selected just one possibility, and the rest of the DPP endorsed it. Why did the DPP elevate this one option? If Sheehan wants to refer to the grapevine in the Schull area, he should gather convincing evidence of its efficiency regarding the murder. Failing that, there should be no idle speculation. If that could not be done, say nothing.

S11

APPENDIX **4**

The remaining DPP sections

1. Lack of Forensic Evidence linking Ian Bailey to the murder scene.

There is no DNA at the moment. There was none at the time of the report. and none may ever be found. The absence of DNA evidence is not evidence of innocence. For centuries, people have been correctly found guilty of murder without forensics. Evidence. Many contemporary murders and serious crimes are still solved without forensic evidence,

The centrepiece of this short section was Sheehan's assertion that Bailey 'volunteered' to give forensic samples to the investigators, which is 'objectively indicative of innocence.'

> "on 10 February 1997 while in custody Bailey willingly gave a sample of blood for analysis. At law he was under no obligation to do so. "
>
> "If Bailey had murdered Sophie, he would have known that there was a definite possibility of forensic evidence such as blood, fibres, hair or skin tissue being discovered at the scene. His voluntary provision of fingerprints and a specimen of his blood is objectively indicative of innocence."

Bailey gratefully embraced Robert Sheehan's assertions, which are often repeated by Bailey's dwindling advocates. What these points actually illustrate is 1. A debatable interpretation of the law 2. A failure to grasp the facts of the case 3. Limited critical thinking 4. A zealous desire to announce Bailey's innocence from the start.

First, the 1990 Criminal Justice (Forensic Evidence) Act states that a member of the Garda Síochána may take a variety of samples for the purpose of forensic testing. These would include samples such as blood, pubic hair, urine, nails, and saliva. One of the stipulations is that a sample my only be taken with the authorisation by a member of the Garda Síochána with a rank of superintendent or higher.

This means that AGS had avenues available whether Ian Bailey willingly or reluctantly gave forensic samples. It is not beyond the realms of possibility that Bailey was told, one way or another, that samples would be taken. In this case, he acquiesced rather than 'volunteered.' Knowing that he could likely be forced to give samples, Bailey gave them. That is hardly an objective indication of innocence.

In Bailey's case, a thorough reading of the files shows us the following comments in Garda Desmond Prendergast's statement (354). It gives the timeline for Ian Bailey's interview on 10.02.1997. He makes two salient points regarding the issue of taking samples.

> "I informed Ian Bailey that he was being detained under section 4 of the Criminal Justice Act 1984 for the proper investigation of the offence for which he was arrested."
>
> "At 4.34p.m. Superintendent J.P. Twomey Bantry gave authorisation for the taking of Blood from Ian Bailey under the Criminal Justice (Forensic Evidence) Act, 1990. "

These facts suggest that Bailey was not the innocent 'volunteer' presented by Sheehan. This was meant to be a balanced analysis and presentation of the facts. It is hard to have confidence in the rest of the report when key points are omitted. In the context of the Prendergast statement, the claim of "objectively indicative of innocence." does not stand up. The concern here is that Sheehan did not refer to the Prendergast statement. It is an unacceptable omission. One must wonder why essential facts were omitted as Sheehan seeks to announce Bailey's innocence,

3. Detention of Jules Thomas allegedly on suspicion of committing the murder

At the heart of this section was Sheehan's assertion that Jules Thomas's arrest and interrogation were unlawful.

> "It would appear that her arrest and detention was unlawful."

> "The detail of her questioning indicates that she was arrested to obtain information which could be used against Bailey. Her detention cannot be legally justified."

He makes this statement not once but twice—he could have made it a dozen times—and it would remain untrue. Sheehan states that the arrest cannot be legally justified. He is wrong. It can be legally justified. Furthermore, it has never been found to be unlawful since. He said it was unlawful rather than that it may be unlawful, which is also untrue. That a lawyer writing such a report makes such statements with conviction when they are merely his opinions is indefensible.

First on the issue of 'voluntary' versus compelled provision of forensic samples, next alleged unlawful detention, there is no justification for taking Bailey and Thomas's side or for excluding important information.

> "She states in the interview with apparent conviction that she is convinced of his innocence."

It is unclear why Thomas's opinions concerning Bailey may be considered relevant to the objective of the report. It is pitiful that Thomas saying something with apparent conviction makes it any more true. It creates the impression that the author was either out of his depth or keen to push a narrative with no evidence to back it up. It is a matter of record that Thomas provided false information to investigators. She supported a false alibi. No doubt she did it with conviction. She said she was convinced he was innocent but could not account for where he was when Sophie was murdered.

Thomas remained with Bailey despite regular bouts of abuse. She made excuses for him. When savagely beaten and hospitalised, she did not press charges. Her excuses and reasons for not pressing charges were undoubtedly done with conviction. A balanced report required a broader context than was offered here. The content of this section provides no basis for deciding whether Bailey should be charged. This section appears to be a way of criticising of An Garda Síochána and little else. The notion that Thomas was arrested only to get at Bailey was untrue.

5. Premonition.

Ian Bailey claimed to have some premonition with dark foreboding. In the DPP report, Robert Sheehan spends most of this section referring to dogs barking and howling earlier in the evening. In part, this is a distraction for both AGS and DPP. The most salient issue is why Bailey took a different route home and stopped at a place that overlooks the eventual crime scene. He then got out of the car and looked toward the Dreenane cottages, including the holiday home of Ms Toscan du Plantier. Bailey failed to explain why he did this.

Rather than focus on a 'premonition,' the other issue is why Bailey originally lied to investigators. He made no mention of stopping. Instead, he claimed he drove straight home. This deception might not be apparent to readers of the DPP report as Sheehan did not mention Bailey's lies about his journey home.

7. Unreliability of Marie Farrell

Over twenty years after the DPP report was written, it is fair to say that Farrell is no longer considered a reliable or believable witness. It is still worth looking at what the report said about her evidence.

Sheehan rightly pointed out that Farrell's statements about the height and appearance of the man she saw were inconsistent. This issue was not a sufficient reason to reject all of Farrell's observations. Farrell said she saw Bailey on December 22nd while driving to Cork City. Sheehan writes about Bailey being at the Murphy household from the 21st to the 22nd of December, claiming that he was not where Farrell said she saw him.

Once again, Sheehan fails to provide all the evidence. While writing about when Bailey was with the Murphys, he forgets to mention that Bailey initially lied through his teeth. He said he was at the Prairie all that night and cut down a Christmas tree the following morning. These are lies from start to end. Yet Sheehan misses it all out. He never addressed address why Bailey lied. What was he hiding or covering up? So often in this report, things are left out, and questions are not even asked, never mind answered.

Despite Sheehan's best efforts, Bailey has no alibi for where he was at 7.15 am on 22.12.1996. Where Farrell saw him would be where one would go to thumb a lift out to the Prairie cottage; it is a little more than a 5-minute walk from the Murphy home. The truth is we don't know, and Sheehan did not know. So, no conclusive inference can be drawn. This did not stop him.

Sheehan sought to cast doubt on Farrell's evidence by claiming she saw him in the dark. She initially gave the statements anonymously, which were not made immediately after the events. All of these are possible. It is also possible that none of them apply. There is insufficient evidence to draw conclusive inferences. It is more like a fishing expedition than an intelligent analysis.

At the end of this report section, Sheehan makes the following point. This point was so important to Sheehan that he raised it twice in different report sections. Both times, it was a lamentable point. He referred to Bailey being seen at Keelfadda Bridge in the early hours of December 23rd.

> " Even if the identification was definite this would be of little probative value given the location was not even indirectly en route between the scene of the murder and Bailey's home."

This is built on the bizarre assumption by Sheehan that Bailey must only be seen on the route from Dreenane to the Prairie cottage! He could have been going to a different place; maybe he parked his car well away. A drunk man who had murdered a woman in a frenzied attack may have an 'amygdala hijack'. The hijack happens when visceral emotions completely override any rational thinking. There are many other potential explanations. We do not know, and more importantly, Sheehan could not know. Nor could he reasonably draw that inference. This means his conclusion is no more than his personal opinion. That was not good enough.

12. Knowledge of injuries to body of deceased.

This was a brief section in the report, and Sheehan primarily refers to damage to Sophie's hand. This leaves out significant issues that may indicate that Bailey did have guilty knowledge that only the murderer or someone close to the murderer would know. Sheehan concluded:

> "A substantial amount of gossip occurred on the day itself about the murder as to how Sophie was killed and in the days and weeks thereafter there was national media speculation in relation to it, her injuries, the murder weapons etc.
>
> An Garda Síochána

From December 23rd, 1996, to the beginning of February 1997, Ian Bailey worked long and hard for several newspapers and publications. He appeared to be producing articles daily under his name or as Eoin Bailey and providing information to other writers. While doing so, he seemed to have access to information that no other journalist could source—information that the Police and Pathologist either did not have or were not disclosing.

On December 24th, 1996, the Irish Examiner published an article by Eddie Cassidy reporting that Sophie " may have been sexually assaulted," adding that AGS was "expecting Harbison to confirm Sophie was sexually assaulted." The prevailing view was that there had been some form of sexual attack. The autopsy was carried out from 1.57 pm on the 24th. Given the extent of the injuries, this would have been a lengthy process. The samples taken would have been unlikely to be analysed until the 26th at the earliest. Some results would not be known for weeks. It is highly improbable that the pathologist could say for sure there had or had not been a sexual assault for several days.

An article by Bailey appeared in the Star newspaper on the 26th. It was a morning newspaper. He wrote, " A post-mortem examination showed she died from multiple head injuries but was not sexually assaulted." The issue here is a simple one. When was the copy submitted to the Star, and when did Bailey acquire this information?

One option was that Bailey knew how he murdered Sophie and that he did not sexually assault her. No one in the Police or forensic services could know unequivocally that there had been no sexual assault this early on in the investigation.

In another article, Bailey wrote:

> "Miss Du Plantier may have held the most vital clue of all in the palm of her hand as she lay dying in the boreen beside her house. "She had a clump of hair in her hand from the head of the attacker. Traces of skin were also found under her fingernails, suggesting she scratched her attacker in a desperate fight for life."

The traces of hair were a closely guarded secret. How did Bailey know about this information? The hair was from Sophie's head and got there as she tried to protect her head from the repeated blows. Elsewhere, Bailey revealed that Sophie had been attacked from behind. This was a detail known only to leading investigators and the pathologist. The Police keep certain information secret as this can be helpful when identifying perpetrators.

Sophie's body was found face upwards. No attacks to the back of her head were found at the scene of the crime. The blunt force trauma to the back of her head only became apparent much later. The final detailed post-mortem report, including the attack to the back of the head, was finished in March. Ian Bailey already knew it. There was never any indication that Bailey had sources for his articles.

14. Fire on the Thomas property.

The issue of fires burning 'rubbish' at the Prairie cottage and studio appears difficult to resolve. To a large extent, it comes down to who a jury might believe. Strangely, Sheehan finds it difficult to reach that conclusion. He appears determined to challenge the statements of people who challenge Bailey. He resorted to a claim that after four months, her recollection could easily be in error as to the date.' However, her recollection could be very accurate. A fire on Boxing Day immediately after Christmas may be a rare occurrence so more memorable. Or maybe Louise Kennedy is more likely to remember events on Boxing Day. Sheehan has no idea about Kennedy's memory. The most telling point here is Sheehan picks a narrative that supports Bailey.

16. General

"A prosecution against Bailey is not warranted by the evidence". This was a lamentable conclusion that condemned Sophie's family to decades of suffering.

APPENDIX **5**

Some questions for Jules Thomas

A thorough review of the evidence results in some important questions for Jules Thomas.
1. Why did she give a false account to investigators of her journey from the Galley bar to the Prairie cottage in the early hours of 23.12.1996?
2. Ian Bailey gave the same false account for that journey. Did she collude with him regarding their statements?
3. Why did she completely change that account of the journey?
4. Ian Bailey gave the same second version of the journey. Did she collude with him regarding the second account?
5. Why did she give Bailey a false alibi for the period between 1 am and 8 am on 23.12.1996?
6. What caused her to withdraw her assertion that Bailey was in bed with her all night?
7. Does she know what he was doing while she slept?
8. Why did she put up with so many beatings from Bailey?

9. Ian Bailey conceded that he was told the victim was a non-national, possibly French; why did you go directly to Dreenane?
10. In separate telephone calls, Ian Bailey told two newspaper men he had been at the crime scene in Dreenane from around 10.30 am to 11. am. On the 23rd, from 11 am to 11.30 am, you told James Camier Bailey was doing newspaper work concerning a murdered French woman at Dreenane. Who told you about the murder before you met with Camier?
11. You told Saffron about the murder before noon on the 23rd. Was it Ian Bailey who told you about the murder on the morning of the 23rd?
12. Did he tell you it was an accident or an unfortunate incident rather than a murder?
13. Were you surprised at the severity of Bailey's attack on Ms Toscan du Plantier?
14. Regarding the scratches, why did you, your daughters, and Bailey give so many contradictory accounts of –
    - When the tree was chopped down?
    - When the turkeys were killed?
    - When were the turkeys delivered and by whom?
    - Who was involved in aiding Bailey with the tree and turkey tasks?
15. Regarding the injuries allegedly suffered by Bailey before the evening in Schull on the 23rd, which of the versions do you think was correct?

Printed in Great Britain
by Amazon